Love Buds

Cooking with Cannabis
By L.B. Cheryl

Cooking with Cannabis is a new and unique style of consuming healthy and healing foods and spices including cannabis.
These healing foods, herbs and spices added into your daily diet can help to ensure optimum health and improve symptoms due to disability or medical conditions.

When prepared in creative ways, healthy food can be fun and delicious. While you are enjoying your culinary experience, I encourage you to utilize the added support from our web site and blog. While the print version has some limitations, our website does not. "What's cooking" is filled with step-by-step preparation tips, photos to help with the process as well as new great recipes added weekly.

Thank you for joining "Cooking with Cannabis"

Cheryl

Copyright © 2015 L.B. Cheryl

All rights reserved.

ISBN-13: 978-0692549308
ISBN-10: 0692549707

Acknowledgements

I really need to thank all my friends, family and salon clients for enduring my two-year obsession with this book. But mostly, I need to thank the following:

My husband, Tom, has been extremely patient. For 17 years he has grown accustomed to me being around the house on my free days from work, enjoying our home, gardens, kids and pets. Once I began this journey of cooking with cannabis and all the different directions it took me, I was almost never home. When I was it was in the kitchen, conjuring recipes or on my computer, writing.

When I cooked, it was nearly always test foods. On top of that, the garden grew weeds and the house collected dust, and I was mostly too tired to socialize with friends. So I say to you Tom, I love you and thanks for your patience and support.

I knew going into this project that it would require some specialized outside help. My entire life is filled with creative work and play; I have few skills in the areas of writing and computers. My thanks go out to my daughters Krista and Kelle for their attention to detail while editing my recipes and the many emergency calls for help.

Kaila Jacobs, my friend and professional editor: Thanks for all the research and format direction to get this book on its way.

My good friend and professional photo shop editor Sandi Fotofixes. Thank you for the many hours of photo editing, computer support and caring friendship.

For all the many people that had a hand in this book, thank you.

Table of Contents

5. INTRODUCTION
   OUR MISSION
6. ABOUT THE AUTHOR
7. MEDICAL DISCLAIMER
8. CANNABIS, HEMP, CBD, THC
9. COOKING WITH CANNABIS

PART I: FOOD & LIFESTYLE

CHAPTER 1: SUPER FOODS & NUTRITION
13. FOOD PAIRING
14. THE MEAT & POTATO DIET
    FOOD PAIRING AND THE SANDWICH
15. NUTRITIONAL COMPONENTS OF FOOD
17. PREPARE FOR A BETTER LIFE
    LOVE BUDS CANNABIS COLLECTION
    HOW TO PURCHASE FROM THE LOVE BUDS COLLECTION
18. SET YOURSELF UP FOR SUCCESS

CHAPTER 2: THE BASICS OF LOVE BUDS AND QUICK REFERENCE RECIPES
19. LOVE BUDS COLLECTION
21. LOVE BUDS SPICE BLENDS
23. **MAKE AT HOME SPICE BLENDS**
24. ORGANIC SMOOTHIE & JUICE POWDERS
25. LOVE BUDS TEA COLLECTION
29. THE BASICS: PREPARING CANNABIS FOR INFUSION WITH FATS, BUTTERS, GHEE & OILS
31. PREPARING SPICE BLENDS FOR INFUSIONS
33. ALCOHOL INFUSIONS BASICS

CHAPTER 3: FOOD LIST
35. BEVERAGES
39. DAIRY
40. EGGS
43. FATS
45. NUTS & SEEDS
47. FRUITS
53. GRAINS & RICE
55. LEGUMES, BEANS & SOY
57. PROTEINS
58. FISH & SEAFOOD
59. SPICES
64. SWEETENERS
67. VEGETABLES

PART II: HEALTH

CHAPTER 4: CHOOSING FOODS FOR VARIOUS HEALTH CONDITIONS
76. ANTI-AGING, ALZHEIMER'S, BRAIN & MEMORY FUNCTION
77. ANXIETY, BI-POLAR DISORDER, DEPRESSION & INSOMNIA
78. CANCER AUTOIMMUNE ILLNESS & NAUSEA
80. DIABETES & SUGARS
82. EYE HEALTH
83. GASTROINTESTINAL, CONSTIPATION, DIVERTICULAR, GALLBLADDER HEALTH, OBESITY & WEIGHT LOSS
85. HEADACHES & MIGRAINES
86. HEART HEALTH, BLOOD PRESSURE, CARDIOVASCULAR & CHOLESTEROL
87. IBD, IBS, CHRON'S DISEASE
88. IMMUNE SYSTEM, AIDS, ANEMIA, HIV, HEPATITIS & HERPES
89. WOMEN HEALTH ISSUES, CHOLESTEROL, HEART, HORMONES, MENOPAUSE, PMS, REPRODUCTION, UROLOGY
91. MEN'S ISSUES
    BLOOD PRESSURE, CHOLESTEROL, HEALTHY HEART, PROSTATE, TESTOSTERONE & UROLOGY
93. NERVE DISORDERS, FIBROMYALGIA, MS, PARKINSON'S & SEIZURES
94. PAIN, INFLAMMATION & OSTEOARTHRITIS
96. RHEUMATOID ARTHRITIS
97. SENSUAL STIMULANT & MOOD BOOST
98. WEIGHT GAIN, ANOREXIA, ENERGY & STAMINA

PART III: THE RECIPES
103. CHAPTER 5: KITCHEN PANTRY
    DRESSINGS, SAUCES & MARINADES
104. VEGAN, GF, GRAIN-FRIENDLY
120. CREAMY COOKING BASICS
122. CREAMY DRESSINGS & TOPPINGS

136. CHAPTER 6: HYDRATION AND LIBATIONS
137. COFFEE AND CHOCOLATE
140. COCKTAIL HELPERS
141. ALCOHOL INFUSIONS
142. SPECIALTY COCKTAILS
145. GREEN JUICES & SMOOTHIES
151. FRUIT, VEGETABLE JUICES & SMOOTHIES
158. TEA

160. CHAPTER 7: BRUNCH WITH A PUNCH
162. BREAD
165. CREPES & PANCAKES
168. CRACKERS
172. OATMEAL & ROLLED OATS
174. DAIRY
    176. **EGGS**
    180. CREPES (WHEAT FREE)
    182. FRIED
    185. QUICHE
    187. SCRAMBLED
    188. STEAMED
189. SALADS
    190. FRUIT AND VEGETABLE SALAD
    194. PROTEIN SALAD
198. STARCH: GRAINS, RICE & QUINOA
199. SANDWICHES & SNACKS TO GO

202. CHAPTER 8: NUTS ABOUT NUTS
204. SALT & SAVORY
208. HONEY NUTS

213. CHAPTER 9: THE DINNER TABLE
214. BACON
215. POULTRY
218. BEEF
220. WILD GAME
221. LAMB
    222. **FISH & SEAFOOD**
226. BEANS & LEGUMES
230. HOT VEGETABLES
    234. **GREEN SUPER FOOD**
    237. **MIXED VEGETABLES**
    243. **SQUASH & POTATOES**
250. TOMATOES
251. PASTA
254. RICE

257. CHAPTER 10: DESSERTS
259. SPECIALTIES
265. CHERRIES & CHOCOLATE
269. FROSTINGS & FILLINGS
272. JAMS
277. PIE CRUST
280. POPSICLES
281. YOGURT PARFAITS
284. WHIPPED CREAM

287. REFERENCE LIST

Introduction
Love Buds: Cooking with Cannabis

Love Buds: Cooking with Cannabis is a beautifully illustrated, easy to navigate collection of recipes, including 250 of the top nutritious foods, herbs and spices for healthy meal preparation. Cooking with cannabis can be tricky, but with Love Buds by your side, the meal planning is safe and easy.

What are Love Buds? Love Buds are organic, nutritious, packaged spice blends with cannabis. We make it simple by combining only the finest ingredients with medical-grade cannabis, spices and herbs that, together, help you manage your health concerns and challenges.

These recipes are for all levels of culinary abilities. They will show you just how easy it is to prepare foods using *Canna Spice Blends*. However, we've also made it possible for you to mix your own spice blends and add cannabis as you want or need to. Be careful that you choose the right strain of cannabis for your particular situation. For helpful information on the different strains, see http://www.leafly.com.

The recipes are equally divided: there are quick and easy recipes for those with moderate ability, and more exotic recipes for the gourmet chef.

These tasty meals are good for you, completely organic and nutritious and will support both common and unusual health issues and concerns.

Tips and Recommendations sections
"Tips and Recommendations" contain interesting notes throughout the book about specific group of foods, spices, fats and teas that needed a little more explanation.

Our Mission: At Love Buds we promise to provide exceptional products and service for those intending to use cannabis in a healthy and safe fashion. It is important at Love Buds to stay healthy, use cannabis wisely and maintain a high-functioning lifestyle. Toward this end, we provide an easy-to-follow nutrition plan that supports your optimum health.

We combine healing herbs and spices with very specific strains of cannabis. At Love Buds, we understand that people have many different needs and wants. Our spice blends include a variety of CBD and THC blends. These *Canna Spice Blends*, combined with specific food pairing, will insure the best possible results when your goal is to feel better and enjoy a productive lifestyle. For more on these components of marijuana and what they mean, see http://www.cascadealt.org/cbd-thc-cbn-thcvs.

About the Author

Cheryl owns a salon specializing in anti-age consulting and treatment, is an artist, and loves cooking and gardening. For some years, she went through an unusual number of health problems including cancer and neck injuries from two auto accidents. Pain finally caused her to obtain a medical marijuana card for relief. However, she didn't like smoking and wanted to find an alternative. When one of her dogs became ill, Cheryl seriously began to research the health benefits of cannabis, seeking relief for her pet. Her search led her to seek recipes and eventually to create her own recipes so people needing the relief that cannabis could provide did not have to smoke it. Eventually she began growing her own strains of marijuana to ensure she had the right strains and the right mix of CBD and THC and other components in the meals she prepared. She is glad to present the results of years of research and experimentation in the kitchen to her readers.

"Today," Cheryl says, "I enjoy nutritional conjuring in the kitchen, working with clients in the salon, gardening, oil painting, playing with and training our dogs. The best parts of my life are my children and my loving husband, Tom. To visit a piece of our life, enjoy a stroll through our websites and keep an eye out for upcoming Cooking with Cannabis volumes.

Pets Love Buds™ Cookie and Crackers

Cooking with Cannabis Collection:
Vol. 1 Healthy Healing Recipes
Vol. 2 French Chef
Vol. 3 Cocktail Party
Vol. 4 Smoke and Grill
Vol. 5 Healthy Pets
Vol. 6 Brunch
Vol. 7 Decedent Deserts
Vol. 8 Chocolate

Vol. 9 Pot Pies
Vol.10 Roasted
Vol.11 Pot and Pasta
Vol.12 Holidays
Vol.13 Easy Crock Pot Meals
Vol.14 Learn to Cook Easy Recipes
Vol. 15 Appetizers and Snacks
Vol. 16 Eat Your Greens

Love Buds: Organic Healthy Healing:
Nutritious and Tasty

By choosing the Love Buds nutritional life style plan you may find the following conditions are improved, or that symptoms are lessened and treatments have fewer side effects. Please see notes below. **

Diabetes: lower blood sugar
Weight loss: belly fat • appetite control
Lowered blood pressure • lowered cholesterol
Anti-aging effects: antioxidant • anti-inflammatory
Increased endorphins: improved mood and well-being
Men's health: mood • prostrate • urinary tract • sexual stability
Improved gastrointestinal health: bowel • colon • intestines • stomach
Women's health: menopause • new mama • PMS • reproduction • hormones
Lowered risk of heart disease and related problems such as vascular damage
Multiple Sclerosis symptoms: depression • cramps • muscles • nerves • tremors
Alzheimer's, dementia: better brain function • Improved memory, mental sharpness
Arthritis and Rheumatoid Arthritis: joint pain • inflammation • stiffness
Parkinson's disease: Lessen seizures, tremors, and cramping
Bi-polar condition: mood swings • depression • energy
Lower blood sugar, blood pressure and cholesterol

Energy problems: lethargic • loss of stamina
Immune system support: hepatitis, AIDS, HIV
Eyesight: glaucoma • macular degeneration
Improve activity and energy, including libido
Migraines headaches: lessen severity or eliminate

Cancer symptom and treatment relief: depression • nausea • nerves • pain • stamina
IBD, IBS (Irritable Bowel Disease or Syndrome; Crohn's disease: constipation • diarrhea

A note to our readers: the dietary information and recommendations in this book are just that: they are not medical advice, and we do not claim that there is medical advice in this book. We are presenting the results of our own research and that of many others, and have noted our sources throughout the book for your verification. Please be sure that if you make dietary changes or change the supplements you might be taking – including cannabis – you should consult with your doctor. There are supplements which interact with prescription drugs or which may not work for your particular set of circumstances. We ask all our readers to treat this information and these recipes with the highest amount of personal responsibility. Above all, please know we present this information and these recipes with a mind toward your optimum health and have not been created for the purpose of getting high.

Cannabis, Hemp, CBD and THC

Hemp is an Asian herb and is the plant from which cannabis is made - but it is not the same as cannabis. Although it claims to have some health benefits, it ranks lower on the healing scale. To understand hemp, see http://www.leafscience.com.

CBD's are the primary healing portion of the cannabis, the "feel-good" that is possible without getting high. There are many other compounds in cannabis.

THC is the most reliable and healing medication but is also the component responsible for causing the familiar marijuana "high." We have found that a complete balance of CBD and THC is the best choice for healthy, healing and productive living.

Love Buds Cannabis Collection

The selections of cannabis used in the Love buds *Canna Spice Blends* are very specific. We grow a selection of organic cannabis to produce varying levels of CBD, THC, THCV and CBG (other healing compounds in cannabis). Because the goal is to help support good health and a sense of wellness, it is critical to have many different varieties. Today we use select blends of cannabis to obtain the correct balance to provide relief and help for a number of health conditions and concerns.

We recommend using small amounts of cannabis in recipes throughout the day rather than a large amount all at once, unless you are seriously ill or have severe chronic pain. If this is the case, you may want to follow the Love Buds Plan and subsidize with additional cannabis of your choice.

The *Canna Spice Blends* have been tested in many different ways. Combining *Canna Spice Blends* with fats and proteins are always the top choice due to the fact that the benefits of cannabis increase enormously when combined and heated with fats and proteins. When cannabis is combined with a nonfat ingredient it provides benefits, but at a lower level than when combined with fats. Any time cannabis is ingested with protein; the benefits are stronger and last longer. When you prepare recipes with little to no heat or no fat, less than half of the healing benefits will be present.

Because cannabis has a rough flavor on its own, it helps to use a little extra sea salt and pepper in some recipes, a little sweetener in others.

Simmering Canna Spice Blend with onions, garlic & chicken broth

Cooking with Cannabis

Here are some guidelines that may help you to enjoy your culinary experience and the effects that follow. Cooking with cannabis is tricky and can smell and taste odd, so heavier, spicier dishes might serve better. For cannabis edibles to work at their peak they must be combined with heat or fermented with some form of fat or alcohol. See the Food Pairing section in Ch. 1, pg. 13. The best fats to use are whole milk or heavy cream, butter, chicken or beef broth, coconut oil, olive oil or seed oil. Combine your chosen herb and fat and heat at a low temperature of 200°-250° for no less than 20 minutes (your mixture may be heated at this low temperature for up to 8 hours). Cooking over high heat for too long can degrade fats as well as the cannabis, especially the THC.

Tips & Recommendations:

- When choosing from a Love Buds recipe, keep in mind the stronger ingredient flavor camouflages the cannabis aroma and flavor. If you prefer not to taste the cannabis, increase the flavor strength.

- Most recipes in the love buds cook book are healthy; if you have no specific food requirements or allergies you can enjoy the entire collection.

- When a recipe contains an ingredient that you are allergic to or don't tolerate well, simply substitute it with a safe choice. You'll find ingredients here that are fun to try as substitutes.

- Note that several of our family lifetime favorite recipes are *not* healthy. But they are included so that when you decide to have a cheat day or a day off from nutrition, you can enjoy our favorites.

Every recipe developed at Love Buds is to support a healthy eating plan. Our recipes may have a lower dose cannabis than what you are accustomed to. Our goal is to help you feel better, but still remain productive. Again, add cannabis as needed.

At Love Buds, we are after the best in wellness performance. With different concerns and ailments to support, we have found that each and every one needs a different level to find relief. While CBD helps with some concerns, THC has a very important role for others. We created blends to suit the specific conditions and concerns, and at the same time support the choice with specific food ingredients. When you purchase from the Love Buds Collection, we recommend that you also try our other varieties to see what might work best for you.

Because our *Love Buds Spice Blend* has 2 teaspoons of Love Buds Cannabis for each 4 servings, you may need to subsidize with a little more cannabis if you need more effect.

Eating vs. Smoking

At Love Buds we do not support smoking in any fashion. We are health advocates so consider it sacrilegious to drag smoke or any kind of carcinogen into your lungs and possibly cause even more damage to your precious body.

When you eat cannabis it acts differently in the bloodstream and in the body than it does when inhaled through smoking or vaporizing. Eating cannabis results in a more physical sensation or body high. This is very good for soothing sore muscles, easing pain, aiding in digestion, and helping with insomnia. It will also provide feelings of warmth and pleasant tingling.

Because everyone's tolerance is different, it's best to start out slowly. Eating cannabis instead of smoking or "vaping" takes a little longer to feel results, so be patient. If you eat too much too soon, you might feel adverse effects. If they are really strong adverse effects, they might include things such as paranoia, dizziness, panicky feelings, hunger, laziness or its reverse, hyperactivity. If you need to take a break, lie down, breathe deeply, listen to music that you love and rest until the feelings pass.

How to start:

First make a list of your personal health concerns, highest to lowest. Using the Love Buds food list and colored markers, underline each ingredient or idea you will use in your daily life plan. The following pages contain some basic nutrition and food information.

NOTES
_____
_____
_____
_____
_____
_____
_____
_____
_____
_____
_____
_____
_____
_____
_____
_____
_____
_____
_____

Chapter 1: Super Foods & Nutrition

Food Pairing

Here are some basic explanations to help you get started

It is imperative to follow correct food pairing. When foods are paired correctly, your system will process the food for the highest nutrient value instead of processing it as sugar and storing it as fat. However, if a meal is lending itself to being digested as sugar, don't worry; quickly eat a small portion of a clean protein and vegetable; follow with plenty of water.

In the beginning food pairing can be a bit confusing, but it does get easier.

Protein + starch = sugar starch
Rice and grain + milk = sugar starch
Rice and grain + any fats = sugar starch

Pair starchy foods (including starchy vegetables) with vegetables for the body to digest them as nutritional fuel.

Protein + vegetables = nutritional fuel
Rice and grain + skim milk = nutritional fuel

When eating protein and/or fats with non-starchy vegetables only, the body digests them as nutritious fuel.

Fruit mixed with anything turns everything to sugar.
When you eat protein or fat with starch or fruit, it digests like sugar.

Food pairing examples for protein and vegetable meals:
Steak and cauliflower mash are great substitutes for potatoes; pair with a side salad with ranch dressing
Barbeque wings and veggies with real blue cheese or ranch dip
Fish served on a bed of sautéed kale and side vegetable
Tofu sauté with peanut sauce over broccoli

Food pairing examples for grains, rice and other starches:
Quinoa or rice with vegetables
Sweet potato or squash and vegetables
Rice, cauliflower and broccoli with fat-free ranch dressing
Oatmeal with fat-free milk and whole grain toast with sugar-free jam
Brown rice with curry vegetable stir-fry and cucumber salad

Food Pairing and the meat and potato diet: Most of us would like to eat a diet rich in meat, potatoes and bread because they are so tasty; they're in the realm of comfort food for a lot of us. But the reality is, they aren't good for you. Even if you do not have weight issues, this combination causes your meal to digest like sugar and to be stored as bad fat instead of good fat. Combining proteins of any sort with starch can only lead to bad things such a high glycemic load, high blood pressure, anxiety, inflammation, cholesterol, migraines, women's and men's hormone symptoms, and more. Protein should be paired with vegetables, and there are a lot of creative ways to prepare them in this book. There are recipes for the most discerning taste.

Food pairing and the sandwich: Aren't sandwiches great? It's too bad that bread, mayonnaise, butter, cheese, and meat combined in any fashion can be a glycemic load nightmare. This combination digests like sugar and goes straight to bad fat. When you need to eat that delicious sandwich, choose spelt bread, mustard, bell pepper, tomatoes, lettuce, salt and pepper.

One way to make this kind of switch is to substitute one ingredient at a time until you get used to fixing sandwiches a different way. Begin slowly with a few kitchen tested favorites such as these: pair meat, fish or poultry with cauliflower, turnip, celery root or parsnip mash, cheese, kale, chick peas, onions or dandelion green chips, vegetable croutons and toppings like jicama.

Remember: The secret to healthy eating lies not only in what foods you eat, but what you eat them with!

Nutritional Components of Food

Amino Acids: These are a must in the daily diet. They are the "chemical units, or building blocks that make up proteins. "They are also the end products of protein digestion, or hydrolysis" (Balch, 2010). Although supplements are available, a portion of the benefits are lost using this method. The amino acids are better absorbed from food. These essential amino acids are found in: beef, chicken, egg whites, elk, kidney beans, lamb, moose, parsley, pork, salmon, seaweed, shellfish, spinach, soy, tilapia, tuna, turkey, veal, watercress, whole grains and white fish.

Antioxidants: As essential factors for healthy eating, antioxidants are "natural compounds that help protect the body from harmful free radicals" (Balch, 2010). Antioxidants fight off atoms (or groups of atoms) that eat away at our healthy cells, creating unhealthy oxidation. They also help to prevent the breakdown of cells that contribute to ailments and disease. Resveratrol is at the top of the antioxidant list and can be found in red wine, dark grapes, peanuts and berries.

Dairy products: Basic dairy products such as milk, cream, cheese and yogurt are included here. Dairy products listed as 1 percent, 2 percent or 3 percent fat actually contain a healthy dose of sugar to make up for the missing fat. Whole milk or raw milk is best. Always chose non-fat or unsweetened whip cream. Use heavy cream because it contains little or no sugar. Non-fat dairy can be paired with rice, grains and starchy foods. Unsweetened whip cream or heavy cream can be used in protein dishes or alone, and can be sweetened with a mixture of stevia and vanilla.

Carotenoids: These are the "fat-soluble pigments found in yellow, red, green, and orange vegetables and fruits. They are a potent family of antioxidants…" (Balch, 2010). These nutrients are better absorbed when paired with foods high in monounsaturated fats, like nuts, avocados and peanut butter.

Cholesterol: This is a substance found in all people and animals, and plays a big role in metabolism and in membrane fluidity. For a healthy body, good cholesterol or HDL (high density lipoproteins) and bad cholesterol, or LDL (low density lipoproteins) needs to stay in balance. The goal is for the good to outweigh the bad while keeping all cholesterol on the lower side. Proper food pairing is critical to keep your heart healthy and keep cholesterol levels low. Although there is medication available to balance cholesterol, a good diet is always the better choice

Fats: There are good fats and bad fats. The body needs fat like an engine needs oil, but we get too much of the bad fats in our diet. These are the saturated fats found in foods such as dairy products and fatty meats such as beef, veal, lamb, pork and ham, and most vegetable oils and palm kernel oil. Fats known as polyunsaturated (corn, soybean, sunflower, some fish oils) or monounsaturated (vegetable and nuts oils such as olive, peanut and canola oils) are healthier than saturated fats, but are still far from healthy. Our recipes include good fats; see Ch. 3, pg. 43. Others are not allowed in the pantry.

Fiber: Fiber is actually a form of carbohydrate and is necessary to help regulate blood sugar, carry food through the digestive track properly, maintain healthy cholesterol and eliminate toxins.

Glycemic Load: This is not to be confused with glycemic index, which is a "scoring system that shows how much glucose appears in the blood after eating a carbohydrate-containing food" (Balch, 2010). A low-glycemic diet can help, prevent, reverse, or postpone diabetes, heart disease, obesity and many other disorders. Fruits and vegetables contain "good sugar" starches, while grains and grain products can contain "bad sugar." The recipes here include some grains that have little impact on your blood sugar level as long as you follow the rules of food pairing.

Omega-3s: These fatty acids are an essential component of healthy nutrition. Omega-3s may not lower cholesterol, but they do keep blood flowing freely. Omega-3s can be found in Flax seed & oil, herring, tuna, salmon, smoked salmon, mackerel, sardines, crab, lobster, scallops, blue fin tuna, oysters, squid, beans, chickpeas, soybeans, tofu, eggs, chicken, white turkey breast, turkey sausage and turkey hot dogs.

Organic foods: They do cost a little more but your food is free of pesticides and is not genetically modified. True organic foods are processed by hand, not machine, and have a higher content of vitamins and minerals - a good investment.

Salt: Composed mostly of sodium chloride, salt is a mineral essential to life and is one of the basic human tastes. The salt used in our recipes is the highest quality sea salt. At home, we balance our diet with 50 percent sea salt, 25 percent kosher salt and 25 percent iodized salt.

Spices and condiments: Fortunately, these are essential parts of a healthy diet. Together, herbs and spices are their own super foods. There are more healthy and healing compounds found in herbs and spices than any other food group. By adding certain spices to your meal plans you can double, if not triple the health benefits.

Tea: Tea is high in vitamins and minerals, and leads the pack as the highest antioxidant, anti-cancer and anti-inflammatory drink around. It also helps to lower blood sugar, cholesterol, and blood pressure, and protects cells from oxidization. Tea can lower the risk of Alzheimer's, stroke, heart attacks, and helps to improve heart, artery and blood vessel function. For more on the health benefits of tea, go to http://www.webmd.com/diet/tea-types-and-their-health-benefits.

Prepare for a Better Life

This schedule is designed to help give you optimum health. We recommend preparing meals and snacks in advance when you can. Many people use the weekend to prepare meals for the week ahead. Remember to take water and snacks with you when you're on the go. Plan for a healthier life and be prepared.

- Eat before you go out and don't arrive somewhere hungry
- Stock your refrigerator and pantry with great healthy foods
- Keep healthy food on hand at all times - in your pocket or purse, your car, at work
- Energy: Try to spend at least 5 minutes each morning outside in a pleasant space with sunlight, breathe deeply. You'll have better energy throughout the day and a more restful sleep at night
- On the road? A travel bag should include fruit, low-sugar, high fiber bars, nuts, veggie tray, protein wraps or bars, a bottle of tea and water

Love Buds Daily Plan

On this plan you'll be eating 6 times a day, half are meals, and half are snacks. Eating healthy meals and snacks throughout the day, in intervals, will keep your blood sugar level, and prevent you from getting too hungry and eating too much at your next meal. The food list contains lots of suggestions on meals and snacks. This plan includes drinking 8 ounces of beverages or water between meals.

Early morning: Be sure to have your first 8 ounces of a beverage: lemon or saffron water, tea, or coffee. Follow with a handful of fruit: blueberries or another kind of non-starchy fruit are recommended.

After breakfast, have a mid-morning snack to keep your energy up. After lunch, eat a mid-afternoon snack to avoid the 3:00 p.m. slump.

After dinner, choose a healthy snack, but no later than two hours before bed.

The goal for each day is:
64 ounces of beverage
4-5 vegetables
4-5 herbs and spices
2-3 protein
2-3 dairy
2-3 tablespoons fats, oils or nuts
1-2 fruits

Set Yourself Up for Success

There are some simple steps you can take to get started with a healthy eating plan. As you try your first cannabis recipes you may find it's best to try things out a little at a time. However, if you're experienced with this kind of cooking, you may want to jump right in. Either way, be patient and experiment with the results. Choose whichever method works for you and will give you the greatest chance of success.

When it comes to food, we believe that if it's junk food (white flour, white sugar, processed foods, fast foods) it's best that it becomes junk in the garbage instead of junk in our bodies. Here are some simple steps:

- **Empty out the fridge and the pantry:** My lovely mother can't throw anything away as she feels it is wasteful. On the other hand, I love to clean out most everything. Cleaning out the pantry and refrigerator is a great first step. Remove the white foods: sugar, flour and rice. Throw out processed foods. Check labels on the following foods for added sugars, preservatives and colorings: breads, bakery items, salad dressings, cereal, dairy, soda, juice, TV dinners, packaged food, chips, pretzels, crackers, and packaged flavored oatmeal. Also get rid of hydrogenated oils, shortening, artificial sweeteners (other than xylitol and stevia), ketchup, sauces, and mixes (cake mixes, boxed and packaged types of mixes).

    If it's too difficult or expensive to start over, start with one or two items at a time. Removing processed sugar and white flour is a really good, small first step. Remember some foods: wheat, corn, potatoes, honey and syrups - have natural sugar and you may need to keep them in limited quantities.

- **Use alcohol only in moderation:** If you are trying to lose weight, it is a good idea to get rid of alcohol until you reach your goal and then continue only in moderation. If it wasn't for the fact that all alcohol turns to sugar in our system, it wouldn't be so bad. Red wine is good for the resveratrol it contains, which delivers huge benefits, but there are other ways to ingest resveratrol as well (dark grapes, cherries, dark berries).

- **Keep good fats, oils and butter:** Be careful how you use and store these. When a fat is on the shelf or in the fridge, it has a rating including omega fatty acids, monounsaturated, polyunsaturated and saturated levels of fat. As fats are heated, the rating and quality changes. For example, olive oil is one of the best fats available but when heated, it breaks down and can become degraded. Please see the oil chart.

So there you have it. Now let's get going towards a healthier life!

Chapter 2: The Basics of Love Buds & Quick Reference Recipes

Love Buds Cannabis spices, teas, infusions

This section displays the spices, teas and infusions which Love Buds offers, along with tips and ideas for using them. You'll find references back to the food list, and the food list provides references to this section.

> **It all begins with spice!**
> Throughout the following pages you will enjoy the many ways in which we use *Canna Spice Blends.* Before we get started, let's talk about the best ways to enjoy Cooking with Cannabis. *Love Buds Canna Spice Blends* were developed to help people enjoy cooking with cannabis in a variety of ways. Using *Canna* Butter and *Canna* Oils are always the most effective and easy-to-use methods for cooking. However, we have provided many other options as well. At any point in this book, you can substitute the butter or oils in recipes with a *Canna* choice. For an added boost of flavor, effect and healing opportunities, heat your *Canna* Spice Blends a few minutes on low before adding other ingredients.

By adding healing spices to your daily meal planning you are magnifying the health benefits of the ingredients. You can choose from our pre-measured spice blends with cannabis or create your own favorite blend. Our splice blends can also be added to any recipe for balanced flavor and easy cooking.

The healing benefits of cannabis, herbs and spices are magnified when heated with fats. To get the most for your *Canna Spice Blends* and to experience the comforting sensations and healing results, precook your herbs and spices with butter or oil as you will see in the recipes.

How much cannabis is in the spice blends?

Each Canna Spice Blend contains approximately 2 teaspoons (or 3 grams) of Spice Blends and 2 teaspoons (or 2-3 grams) of CBD- or THC-balanced cannabis. You will find that most Love Buds recipes were created to serve 4 average sized helpings. 2 teaspoons of Spice Blend are the amount of seasoning used in the Love Buds test kitchen. 2 teaspoons (or 2-3 grams) of CBD or THC balanced cannabis is the equivalent of approximately 2 joints. This analogy is for the purpose of understanding what is in the *Canna Spice Blends;* we do *not* advocate smoking, and know that most people using cannabis for medical reasons prefer not to smoke it as well. The amount of cannabis we use depends in part upon the harvest and the results of tests for potency.

NOTES

Love Buds Spice Blends

All of our spice blends are completely organic & prior to adding cannabis were approved by the **Oregon Department of Agriculture**

Bar-B-Que Spice Blend (salt free) Ingredients: 2 t cannabis, ¾ t tomato, ¾ t onion, ½ t smoke flavor, ¼ t paprika, ¼ t black pepper, ¼ t garlic, ¼ t celery and ¼ t mustard seed, 1 pinch each, lemon peel, allspice, cinnamon and clove.

Savory Beef Spice Blend Ingredients: 2 t cannabis, ¾ t sea salt, ¾ t onion, ½ t garlic, ¼ t sugar, ¼ t nutmeg, ¼ t basil, ¼ t ginger, ¼ t fennel, ¼ t chili flakes, pinch coriander and oregano.

Chili Spice Blend (salt free) Ingredients: 2 t cannabis, 1 t dark roast paprika, 1 t oregano, 1 t cumin, ¾ t garlic, ¾ t cayenne and ¾ t garlic.

Chinese Five Spice Blend (salt free) Ingredients: 2 t cannabis, ¾ t star anise, ¾ t cloves, ¾ t cinnamon, ½ t fennel seed and ½ t black pepper.

Curry Spice Blend (salt free) Ingredients: 2 t cannabis, ¾ t coriander, ½ t turmeric, ½ t cumin, ½ t fenugreek, ½ t cayenne, ½ t black pepper, ¼ t yellow mustard, ¼ t ginger, ¼ t cinnamon, pinch cardamom, cloves and nutmeg.

French Spice Blend (salt free) Ingredients: 2 t cannabis, 1 t basil, ½ t saffron, ½ t rosemary, ½ t thyme, ¼ t parsley, ¼ t marjoram, pinch lavender and tarragon.

Fruit Pie Spice Blend (salt free) Ingredients: 2 t cannabis, 1 t cinnamon, ¾ t ginger, ½ t allspice, ½ t clove and ¼ t nutmeg.

Greek Island Spice Blend (salt free) Ingredients: 2 t cannabis, 1 t oregano, ¾ t garlic, ½ t dill weed and seed, ½ t cinnamon, ¼ t peppermint, ¼ t chili flakes and pinch nutmeg.

Italian Spice Blend (salt free) Ingredients: 2 t cannabis, 1 t garlic, 1 t oregano, ½ t basil, ½ t marjoram and ¼ t sage.

Jamaican Jerk Spice Blend (salt free) Ingredients: 2 t cannabis, ¾ t brown mustard seed, ½ t ginger, ½ t chili flakes, ½ t fennel seed, ½ t garlic, ½ t paprika, ¼ t allspice, ¼ t thyme leaf, ¼ t onion, ¼ t black pepper, ¼ t cayenne powder, pinch cinnamon powder and clove powder.

Spicy Jelly Spice Blend (salt free) Ingredients: 2 t cannabis, 1 t cinnamon, ¾ t ginger, ¾ t red pepper flakes, ½ t allspice, ½ t clove and ½ t nutmeg.

Lemon Pepper Spice Blend (salt free) Ingredients: 2 t cannabis, ½ t black pepper, ½ t onion, ½ t garlic, ½ t lemon, ½ t rosehips, ½ t celery seed, ½ t orange peel, ½ t turmeric, ¼ t savory, and ¾ t parsley flakes.

Pickling Spice Blend (salt free) Ingredients: 2 t cannabis, 1 t dill seed, 1 t yellow mustard seed, ½ t coriander, 1 bay leaf, ½ t cinnamon, ½ t chili pepper flakes, ¼ t allspice, ¼ t ginger, ¼ t black pepper and ¼ t cloves.

Poultry Spice Blend (salt free) Ingredients: 2 t cannabis, 1 t thyme, ¾ t sage, ¾ t marjoram and ¾ t rosemary.

Taco Spice Blend (salt free) Ingredients: 2 t cannabis, ¾ t cumin, ¾ t chili powder, ¾ t garlic, ½ t tomato, ½ t paprika, ½ t onion, ½ t oregano, ½ t cilantro, ½ t yellow mustard and ½ t cayenne.

Thai Spice Blend (salt free) Ingredients: 2 t cannabis, ¾ t chili powder, ½ t coriander, ½ t garlic, ½ t chili flakes, ½ t lemongrass, ½ t lemon peel, ½ t ginger, ½ t star anise, ½ t cilantro, ½ t onion, ½ t basil, pinch cumin, cayenne, white pepper, cinnamon and lemon oil.

Make at Home Spice Blends

Choose from any Love Bud Spice Blend. Add listed ingredients, with the first listed having the greater amount, add until you have a total of 2 teaspoons of spice and 2 level teaspoons of roasted cannabis. Always choose organic, fair trade and fresh spices and herbs for the greatest flavors and healthy healing benefits.

Love Buds
Organic smoothie & juice powders

There's nothing like a refreshing green drink or a smoothie, especially when you know you're packing super healthy ingredients into the mix. Try these for ramping up your health!

Green Power Powder The following ingredients will work to give you a stronger immune system and a much healthier daily life: cannabis, barley grass, wheat grass, spirulina, spinach, alfalfa leaf, kelp, dulse leaf, barley grass juice, orange peel, beet root, dandelion leaf, lemon peel, ginkgo leaf, and wheat grass juice.

Maca Happy Powder This smoothie powder is known for increasing mood, stamina, general health, sexual interest and brain health. Ingredients: cannabis, maca, barley grass, wheat grass, spirulina, spinach, alfalfa leaf, kelp, dulse leaf, barley grass juice, orange peel, beet root, dandelion leaf, lemon peel, ginkgo leaf, and wheat grass juice.

For more complete information about smoothies and juices, see "Beverages" on the food list.

NOTES
_____
_____
_____
_____
_____
_____
_____
_____

Love Buds Tea Collection
All of our Love Buds teas are completely organic

As you know, to get the best results from *Canna Spice Blends* they need to be heated with a fat; as a result, we recommend that you brew your teas with cream. This method will provide the best in tea's healthy qualities. When you add *Canna* Cream to your *Canna* Tea you are doubling the effect and strength of flavor.

Preparing your Love Bud Teas

The tea collection has no added sweeteners or dairy; add as you please. After much testing, this is our recipe of choice:

Combine and whisk 8 cups filtered water and 1 *Canna Tea Blend;* or 2 tablespoons (6 grams) raw tea, 2 teaspoons (2 grams) cannabis and 1 teaspoon stevia, honey or maple syrup.
Bring to a boil, reduce heat and steep 10 minutes.
Add cream and steep 10 more minutes. When using cream, you may like a stronger brew; for black tea, you may like it softer and with a pinch of stevia. With some of the blends, a stronger brew will help camouflage the cannabis taste, if needed.

As with all our recipes, we recommend a little experimentation. As always you will receive a greater benefit from the cannabis if you brew your tea with coconut oil, ghee, whole milk or cream. Store any unused, brewed tea in the refrigerator and dry tea in a cool dark place, sealed.

Mango Black Tea
This is a Fair Trade tea, strong and smooth. An antioxidant, it helps to lower bad cholesterol, is anti-inflammatory, and helps to fight cancer and promote heart health. Ingredients: Black tea, cannabis, calendula marigold petals, and mango flavor.

Chai Tea Blended
This great tea is an aphrodisiac, anti-aging, and anti-inflammatory tea. An antioxidant, it aids digestion, provides fresh breath, and soothes the stomach and gut. Ingredients: Black and green tea, cannabis, cinnamon, cardamom, cloves, fennel, ginger, licorice root and black pepper.

Dandelion Detox Blended Tea
A mild caffeine-free tea, very refreshing. This tea is used as a cleansing agent; aids in circulation to warm up cold hands and feet; and helps to calm down diverticulitis as well as promote a healthy urinary track. Ingredients: Black and green tea, cannabis, burdock, dandelion root, peppermint, red clover, licorice, yellow dock and ginger.

Energy Green Tea A mild and woody antioxidant, this green tea serves as an aphrodisiac, is invigorating and brings greater energy, is a mood-booster and fights depression. In addition, it's healthy for the digestion, arteries and heart; helps to fight cancer, relieve fibromyalgia and arthritis, helps to lowers cholesterol, improve circulation and relieves morning sickness. Ingredients: young Hyson tea, cannabis, eleuthero root, schisandra berry, ginkgo leaf, gotu kola, licorice root and ginger root.

Hibiscus Ginger Lemon Blended Tea This tea soothes stomach and gut irritations, lowers cholesterol, helps to relieve fibromyalgia and arthritis, fights cancer, improves circulation, helps to relieve morning sickness. Ingredients: Black and green tea, cannabis, hibiscus, rosehips, orange peel, lemongrass, ginger, fennel, lemon peel, and lemon oil.

Orange Cinnamon Black Tea Another Fair Trade tea, this relaxing, aromatic tea helps to protect against aging, fights various kinds of cancer, and is antiviral, antifungal and antibacterial. It also helps to lower cholesterol, is anti-inflammatory, strengthens capillaries, lowers blood pressure, and helps fight infections. This tea helps to relieve gas and cramps, and helps with pelvic issues and diabetes. Ingredients: Black tea, cannabis, cinnamon, orange peel.

Red Rose Bud Blended Tea An antioxidant agent and gentle tea which helps support brain health and fight Alzheimer's; an appetite and digestion stimulant; relieves gas and cramps and pelvic issues; anti-bacterial, and helps fight diabetes. Ingredients: Black and green tea, red rose buds and petals, cannabis, Vitamin C, Licorice, spearmint, orange peel, cinnamon, raspberry and lemon.

Relaxing Rose Bud Blended Tea A caffeine-free tea, great for unwinding and relaxing, easing tense muscles, and calming the mind. This antioxidant tea helps relive cramps from PMS, soothes intestinal issues, and is anti-inflammatory. Ingredients: Black and green tea, cannabis, spearmint, lemongrass, elderberry, rose bud, linden flower, chamomile flower, raspberry leaf and orange peel.

Passion Flower White Tea This tea rates highest in polyphenols which help with anti-aging. An antioxidant, it promotes brain health and fights Alzheimer's; helps alleviate cramps, labor pains and works to alleviate many female issues such as PMS, menopause, and pelvic concerns. This white tea is an anti-inflammatory that helps promote gastrointestinal health and also provides immune support. It helps to alleviate insomnia, nervous tension, stress, headaches, and depression. Ingredients: white tea, cannabis and passion flowers.

Jasmine Bud Green Tea: A strong, sharp green tea, this Jasmine tea often serves as an aromatic aphrodisiac, increasing sensual pleasure and overall wellbeing. Ingredients: premium jasmine buds and flowers, cannabis.

French Saffron Black Tea: This rich, deep and flavorful tea lowers bad cholesterol, is an antioxidant, helps fight cancer and promotes heart health. Ingredients: Black tea, cannabis, calendula flowers, mango flavor, lavender, saffron, ginger, basil, rosemary, thyme, parsley, marjoram, tarragon (See saffron and ginger on the spice list for added benefits).

Saffron Ginger Memory Blended Tea: A mild, caffeine-free blended tea; it does just what its name infers; helps boost brain power, and enhance the memory. This tea also lowers cholesterol, increases circulation, relieves symptoms of fibromyalgia and arthritis, helps to alleviate morning sickness, and serves as a sensual stimulant. Ingredients: Black and green tea, cannabis, ginkgo, hibiscus flowers, eleuthero, gotu kola, saffron, ginger, parsley, alfalfa and bilberry.

You can purchase our CBD or THC *Love Buds Spice Blends* with or without the Cannabis at local Oregon dispensaries; or simply order the *Love Buds Spice Blends* and combine them with cannabis that you purchase in your own state dispensary.

Cooking with Canna Tea & Canna Tea Cubes
For an added boost of vitamins, minerals & antioxidants, replace water in recipes with prepared *Canna* Tea. For a boost in your beverage, replace water ice cubes with prepared *Canna* Tea ice cubes.

NOTES

The Basics

Preparing your cannabis for infusion with fats, butter, ghee & oils

There are many methods used to create cannabis butters. With the new scientific research available, how we cook with cannabis is better than ever!

At Love Buds we grind frozen cannabis, taking care not to grind it too fine or it will end up cloudy. Roasting the prepared cannabis prior to cooking will soften the flavor and boost the effects.

Heat your oven to 225°, spread out the ground cannabis on a cookie sheet and bake for 1 ½ hours. To remove the valuable cannabis residue from the grinder and enhance the strength, add 4 tablespoons Everclear® alcohol to the grinder and pulse. Pour and stir the green alcohol into the baked cannabis. Now you are ready to continue with your recipe.

Add one of these choices to 1 lb. of butter or 16 oz. of oil:

At Love Buds, we work with three choices of CBD strong cannabis:
- 3-4 ounces small leaf (CBD averaging 6%-10%)
- 2-3 ounces trim (CBD averaging 9%-13%)
- 1 ounce bud (CBD averaging 10%-15%)

Our THC strong cannabis choices are:
- 2-3 ounces small leaf (THC averaging 10%)
- 1-2 ounces trim (THC averaging 15%)
- ½ ounce bud (THC averaging 20%)

Keep in mind, every harvest yields a slightly different % of CBD and THC.

Tip: You can save the used cannabis residue or "smush" to use in our Love Buds for Pets recipes.

WARNING: Before attempting to make canna butter for the first time, we highly recommend that you try making clarified butter first. When you overcook the butter and get it too brown, the batch will be degraded. It is very important the butter only sizzles (this is water leaving the butter as it simmers) but does not boil. If you overcook a canna batch, the flavor and the health benefits from the butter will be degraded.

Understanding the smoke points for healthy fats & oils

When fats and oils are heated beyond their smoke point they turn to bad fat and the oil is degraded. Choose a fat that has a smoke point 30-50 degrees higher than your intended temperature. Unrefined oils and fats are always cold or slightly warm (room temperature). Choose the correct fat for your preparation method.

High-Searing: bring to high then add ingredients
475°F-Clarified Butter Ghee
465°F-Refined Extra Virgin Light Olive Oil (difficult to find)
460°F-Olive Pomace Oil (difficult to find)
450°F-Peanut Oil
400°F-Walnut, semi refined

Medium High - Stir fry, heat, then add ingredients.
400°F-Light Extra Virgin Olive Oil
375°F-Macadamia Nut Oil
375°F-Extra Virgin Olive Oil

Medium-baking and roasting
350°F-Coconut Oil
350°F-Butter, unsalted: Unsalted butter is recommended for cooking.
325°F-Olive Oil - medium low to medium heat: add ingredients, then set to low
325°F Sesame Oil - best left cold, but some heat is ok: keep below 320°F.
300°F-Butter, salted (burns faster than unsalted butter).
225°F-Flax seed or unrefined cold oils will spoil if heated above 225°F, refrigerate
200°F-Hemp oil - cold oil only, will spoil if heated above 200°F; refrigerate.

As a rule of thumb the lighter the color of the oil or fat – the more transparent it is -- the higher the smoke point. There are other oils that have a high smoke point but they did not make it to the top 300 healthiest foods.

Butter and Ghee
The difference between butter and ghee is the milk solids. When milk is completely removed from butter, it becomes ghee.

Quick Butter
Simmer 1 pound of unsalted butter with 1 ounce CBD rich cannabis for 2 hours; strain, strain, strain, then cool and skim.

Butter
In a small crock pot or stove top sauce pan on low heat, add unsalted butter and cannabis (described above, preparing your cannabis for infusion). Never over-cook. The butter should always be golden brown but never dark brown. Cook for 4 hours to achieve higher CBD and lower THC levels and 8 hours for higher THC, lowering the CBD levels. Cool and strain 3 times (canna smush) and pour through cheese cloth into 1-cup containers with lids. Refrigerate 2 weeks or freeze up to 6 months. Save the smush for dog treat recipes.

Ghee (also known as clarified butter or digestive fire)

Use as a topping or spread, in baking, cooking or frying. Ghee is the healthiest of all butters and fats. In a small crock pot on low, add 2 cups of water, unsalted butter and prepared cannabis (described above). Cook for 4 hours to achieve higher CBD and lower THC levels; or 8 hours for higher THC and lower CBD levels. Cook until the butter turns light brown for the greatest nutty flavor. Cool and strain 3 times (freeze and store the remaining strained *Canna* smush, for later use). Place butter in a bowl in the refrigerator for 24 hours. Skim off all the foam (milk solids), break up and remove solid *Canna* Butter leaving the water. Skin underside of *Canna* Butter blocks (residual watery milk solids and cannabis particles) and put in a separate container for another use (soup base, shakes etc.). Heat *Canna* Butter and pour through cheese cloth into 1-cup containers with lids. Ghee requires no refrigeration, and in fact has even more health benefits if left at room temperature.

Smush
Canna smush is the remaining strained cannabis residual from making butter and infusions. It can be used in other recipes when a diluted effect is desired.

Water
Canna water is the water remaining after making the longer versions of butter and infusions. Use canna water in place of water when an added boost is needed.

Love Buds Canna Butter and Ghee Recipe

We use this recipe the most in Love Buds recipes. Simmer 1 pound of unsalted butter with 1 ounce CBD leafy trim cannabis for 2 hours, strain 3 times, cool and skim. No refrigeration is needed if you skim away all the foamy milk solids, leaving only ghee.

Preparing Canna Spice Blends for infusion

If you are lucky enough to live in a legal state, you can purchase a quick & easy Cooking With Cannabis Infusion Mix

Spiced Butter and Ghee
Follow the same directions as above, adding 1 *Canna Spice Blend* for each 1 cube of butter. With this method there is less cannabis, resulting in a milder batch. Use it for additional flavor and an extra punch of good feelings. If you would like a more powerful cannabis seasoned butter or ghee, simply add more cannabis or an extra *Canna Spice Blend*.

Honey, almond, peanut, or pumpkin butter and ghee:
Add 1 cup honey, almond butter, peanut butter, or pumpkin to 1 cup canna spiced butter.

Canna Oils: coconut, macadamia, olive, peanut and walnut

Combine in a crock pot, 3 parts oil to 1-part cannabis. Choose any high-smoke oil and gently simmer on low heat: do not boil. Stir until some cannabis floats. Use low heat 4-6 hours for a higher CBD level and 6-8 hours for a higher THC level. Heat 1-2 extra hours if the cannabis is fresh and not dried. Cool; strain 3 times. The last strain should be through a fine cheese cloth. Pour cooled oil into an airtight container with a lid. Refrigerate for up to 3 months.

Quick and Easy Oils
Fill a bottle with cannabis plant, then fill to the top with oil. Seal, place in bowl for seepage and let stand for 24 hours and up to 6 weeks; the longer the stronger.

Spiced Oils
(Choose any of our *Canna Spice Blends.*) We love to add an extra kick by adding a little something extra, like 2 tablespoons chili flakes to the *Canna Chili Spice Blend,* and mushrooms to the *Canna Savory Beef Spice Blends.*

Oil of France
Wrap and tie in cheese cloth ¾ ounce cannabis leaf or shake, ½ teaspoon saffron, 2 inches ginger root peeled and sliced and 2 *Canna French Spice Blend*s. Combine with 3 cups of the finest extra virgin olive oil and 3 cups water: cook on low for 6-8 hours. Remove cannabis bag, squeeze (smush) and place the oil in a clean bowl; cool in the freezer for a few hours. Separate the hardened oil from water (save water and freeze). Heat the oil and strain through 2 cheese cloths; strain 2 or more times before storing. The final strain is through an extra fine cheese cloth, not a paper coffee filter. Store this gem in a dark bottle in the refrigerator.

Rose Bud Oil
Wrap and tie in cheese cloth ¾-ounce CBD-rich cannabis leaf or shake (the leafy fragments left behind when sorting) along with 2 *Canna Red Rose Bud Teas*. Add 2 cups of the finest organic coconut oil and 3 cups water. Cook on low for 6-8 hours. Remove cannabis bag, squeeze (smush) and place the oil in a clean bowl; cool in the freezer for a few hours. Separate the hardened oil from water (save water and freeze). Heat the oil and strain through 2 cheese cloths; strain 2 or more times before storing. The finial strain is through an extra fine cheese cloth -- not a paper coffee filter. For a beautiful finish add 2 tablespoons dried red rose buds and pedals. Store this gem in a dark bottle in the refrigerator.

Love Buds Gift Bag
Give this as a gift in a fancy bottle in a pretty sleeve. Use the recipe above, except add 1 nice bud, 1 saffron flower, lavender and ginger, then pour in the infused oil. Seal.

Cold Infusion (vinegars & cold oils like flax)
Follow the Quick & Easy Oil infusion above. Place in a sealed jar and store in the refrigerator for 10 days, shaking daily.

Alcohol Infusions

Here are some quick reference recipes to keep on hand.

Tips & Recommendations:

- At Love Buds, we like all cannabis to be roasted in the oven prior to adding to any infusions or recipes. See Pg.29
- See "Beverages, Pgs. 35-38" in the Food List for additional recipes.
- To prepare flavored cocktails, see "Specialty Cocktails, Pgs. 142-143"
- Find more creative ways to infuse alcohols and create exotic cocktails in the Love Buds Cooking with Cannabis Cocktail Party Cook Book.
- Due to our culinary diversity we like to choose from many different cannabis infusions. We mostly use brandy, Everclear® dark rum, light rum, vodka and whisky. Use these same recipes for any of these varieties.

Alcohol, Cannabis Infusions: 5-10 day recipe

Place 3-4 ounces of leaf, 2 ounces of sweet leaf or 1 ounce of buds in a cheese cloth baggie. Add to a quart of Everclear®, vodka, rum or gin. (Be aware that Everclear® is a much stronger proof alcohol.) Place in freezer, shaking 2 times daily for 5 days, or for 10 days if stored in a dark cool place. Strain and store in a sealed dark glass bottle.

Alcohol, Cannabis Infusion: 10-hour recipe

WARNING!: *While cooking, do not put the lid all the way down; it needs to vent so the pressure doesn't cause an explosion!*

Using 4 parts alcohol to 1-part cannabis leaf, slow cook the mixture on very low heat, about 8-10 hours, stirring occasionally. Continue cooking until the cannabis no longer floats., about 8-10 hours. If using fresh cannabis, it might take 12 hours. Strain, strain, strain. Store it in a cool, dark place.

Always the freshest organic ingredients.

*Whenever possible,
purchase local & garden fresh
for the best nutritional value.*

Chapter 3: Food List

A guide to help you choose the healthiest foods

The following food list includes healthy and nutritious foods used in our recipes. The recipes are presented with the understanding that you already have a good basic knowledge of cooking and following recipes. The recipes you will find in this book are for those interested in optimum health and a long-term life plan, not a quick fix.

This list includes the most valuable foods available to us in the modern world. When you choose to shop and prepare meals and snacks from this list you are choosing a healthy life plan and working toward your own optimum health.

Warning: There are many conditions, including allergies, which mean some people cannot eat some foods on this list. Perhaps something on the list simply does not appeal to you. The choice is yours: what we list here is not a mandate to eat certain items. These are just recommendations. There may be many substitutes for those with allergies and other medical conditions, and for those whose tastes differ.

The foods on this listed appear in order of highest vitamin and mineral content, and the greatest anti-inflammation and digestive benefits.

Beverages

Here are the top 8 beverages to include daily:

Water Drink 6-8 glasses per day. For variety, add any of these ingredients: cucumber, celery and cilantro, lemon, lime, ginger and saffron.

Tea Drink 3-4 cups of tea and coffee each day. Love Buds Tea Blends are not your ordinary off-the-shelf tea bags. Because we care about your health, our organic healing, nutritious and tasty teas are presented to you as organic loose tea that has little processing. Although much more healthy, tea in this form can be bitter and may need a little sweetener to bring out the delightfully soft but bold flavor.

Our creative blending of tea, herbs, spices and cannabis makes our organic Love Buds Tea Blends extraordinarily healthy. Consider the benefits of tea itself: Tea delivers nearly 0 calories, is high in vitamin C and many of the B vitamins; it contains necessary minerals ascorbic acid and folic acid, and is a leading antioxidant, anti-cancer, and anti-inflammatory agent. Tea helps to lower blood sugar, cholesterol, and blood pressure, and protects cells from oxidization stress. Tea can help to lower the risk of Alzheimer's, stroke and heart attacks, and helps improve heart, artery and blood vessel function.

Black tea An oxidized tea with half the caffeine of coffee, but more caffeine than green and white teas. Black tea is the leading tea for reducing LDL's (the bad form of cholesterol), the risk of stroke and heart disease, and for building stronger blood vessels. Black tea is sometimes mistakenly called fermented, when it is actually oxidized. See http://www.eliteabar.com/blogs/tea-education/7564628-tea-oxidation.

Green tea The least-processed and least oxidized tea. It is known for its medicinal powers, including lowering the risk of Alzheimer's, artery disease, cancer, and blood clots. Green tea helps lower blood sugar and is beneficial in weight loss, relaxation, calming the nerves, and boosting one's mood. See http://www.teavivre.com/info/how-to-process-green-tea/.

White tea The super tea! White tea is minimally processed, using tender baby leaves with buds that have not opened yet. It is then withered, or dried. Highest in antioxidants, polyphones and vitamins, white tea delivers the most healing properties with less caffeine than black or green. See http://theteadetective.com/WhiteTeaProcessed

Coffee Everybody's favorite "Morning Joe" has nearly 0 calories and, with its caffeine, acts as a stimulant. It is an antioxidant and helps lowers blood sugar. Two or more cups per day can have a positive effect on blood pressure and can decrease heart disease and PMS symptoms. Four or more cups may help with diabetes and cramps, improve mood, mind clarity, and stamina, and could help with weight loss. Try brewing coffee with ½-decaf and ½-regular, mixing Columbia and French roast.

Fruit and Vegetable Juices:
Have 1-2 cups a day of fresh juice, which serves as an antioxidant and anti-inflammatory agent, and is high in vitamins and minerals. The concentration of vitamins and minerals are especially beneficial for weight loss plans, constipation, irritable bowel syndrome, and immune support.

Super Green Power Powder:
Super Green powder mixes are plant-based concentrates which serve as an alkalizing agent. They may be mixed from a variety of ingredients such as barley grass, wheat grass, spirulina, spinach, alfalfa leaf, kelp, dulse leaf, orange peel, beet root, dandelion leaf, and ginkgo leaf. Green powder drinks are well-known to increase stamina, promote weight loss and mental clarity and boost energy levels. They are easy on the stomach and intestines, and are fat-free. These potent plant foods are complete green supplements loaded with all the vitamins, minerals and enzymes that our bodies need to support optimum health and well-being.

Maca Happy Powder:
The powder comes from the Maca root. A boost for mood, stamina, sexual interest and brain health, this super food also helps relieve chronic fatigue syndrome and enhances energy and memory. Maca powder can help create hormone balance, relieve PMS and menopause symptoms; and helps with weak bones, depression, stomach cancer, leukemia, and a host of other conditions and illnesses.

Aloe Vera:
This popular juice, very high in vitamins and minerals, is well-known for helping to heal skin burns and cuts, but it also helps to heal inflammatory bowel disease, diarrhea and constipation, and helps with heartburn. Some think it could help with yeast infections.

Protein Powder and Protein Drinks, including whey isolate:
Whey Isolate is not a beverage, but is grouped as one due to the average person's method of consumption. For full information on whey isolate, see the dairy section below.

Protein drinks in general help lower stress and blood pressure, aid in weight loss and bone health, and are digested more easily than most other proteins. They are loaded with amino acids, vitamins and minerals, calcium, phosphorus, magnesium and potassium.

Beverage Tips & Recommendations

The recommended fluid intake per day is between 6 and 8 glasses of water. 1-5 cups of coffee or tea. The hydration value of coffee & tea is ½ that of water.

- Begin each day with a glass of fresh lemonade consisting of 12 ounces water, 1 lemon quartered and 1 teaspoon of stevia. One hour later, follow with a handful of blueberries.
- Eat blueberries first thing in the morning to boost your mood hormone; they help cheer you up when you're feeling down, or make a good day even better.
- For a creamy smoothie try adding *Canna* Cream, Ch.6, pg.139.
- Include alfalfa and barley grass in your smoothies and juice.
- A note about fruit smoothies or juice: due to the fiber, sugar and calorie content of fruit mixes, these are considered a food (meal) and not a beverage -- so watch the calories.
- When juicing, it might take a while to discover a favorite recipe. Try these ideas:
    - For a creamy texture add ½ a banana.
    - For a lower calorie smoothie try plain yogurt with stevia.
    - Keep frozen sliced grapes, lemons and limes for attractive edible garnishes.
- Add *Canna* Milk (Ch.6, pg.139) or *Canna* Cream (Ch.6, pg.139) to your coffee for *Canna* Love Buds healing properties

Alcohol Consumption

Most people can enjoy 3-5 cocktails or glasses of wine per week with no problem. For many people there are health benefits. Red wine contains resveratrol, which "might be a key ingredient that helps prevent damage to blood vessels, reduces low-density lipoprotein (LDL – the "bad cholesterol") cholesterol, and prevents blood clots." See http://www.mayoclinic.org/diseases-conditions/heart-disease/in-depth/red-wine/art-20048281.

Dairy

Although dairy is not for everyone, it is important in many diets

Butter is good for you, but be sure you are buying organic, grass-fed cow butter. Butter supports the immune system and contributes to healthy vision; it is loaded with vitamins E, K and D for fighting cancer and building bones. This tasty delight helps fight belly fat and reduces weight, putting it right on our "favorites" list. Include it as you like.

Ghee has had all the milk solids removed from the butter during and following the heating process. Ghee is essential in the fight against inflammation and is lactose-friendly and safe for those with dairy sensitivity. It promotes flexibility and a healthy digestive track, and lowers cholesterol. When ghee is made from grass-fed cows it contains cancer fighting agents, increases fatty acids and aids in weight loss. The anti-aging, antioxidant rewards come from the fight against free radicals. Ghee is known in some societies not as a fat but as a healer. Ayurveda medicine, a holistic, alternative medicine to us but the traditional system of medicine in India, uses ghee for well-being and immunity essential in the stability of mind, brain and the nervous system. No refrigeration is needed due to the absence of milk solids, water or preservatives. Keep ghee in an air-tight container at room temperature for maximum benefits. Ghee tastes great and is loaded in vitamins A, D, E and K.

Cheese Although we do not count calories in this food plan itself, it is still a good idea to keep calories in mind for a weight loss plan. As a result, this list is arranged by calorie count and nutritional content.

> First Choice: 20-50 calories (per serving) ▶ Goat cheese, regular and nonfat cottage cheese, nonfat cheese
>
> Cottage cheese fruit salads are tempting to eat, but it's best to always eat fruit on an empty stomach and not with other foods whenever possible.
>
> Second Choice: 60-70 calories (per serving) ▶ Soy cheese, Ricotta, Feta, Mozzarella and American cheeses
>
> Third Choice: 90 calories (per serving) ▶ Brie, Blue, Provolone, Gouda, Monterey jack and Swiss cheeses
>
> Fourth Choice: 116 calories (per serving) ▶ Havarti, Jarlsberg, Parmesan, Colby and Cheddar cheeses

Cream and Milk Use raw or skim milk, cow milk, goat milk, almond milk and buttermilk. Most milk contains sugar (2% milk, 1% and low-fat milk all contain sugar), so instead choose heavy cream, whole raw milk or nonfat milk. Dairy fat found in heavy cream will naturally digest in the system as a protein because of the absence of sugar. Never add fatty milks to grains or rice or the starch (sugar) will aid the milk fat into digesting like a sugar and not a protein. Skim milk will also digest as a protein. As we all know, properly digested fat is much better for us than sugar.

#1. Choice in Dairy ▶ Fat Free Yogurt: Live active cultures. The probiotic found in Greek yogurt does a better job when paired with bananas and whole grains. This food grouping goes against proper food pairing but in fact does deliver a higher nutritious value. Yogurt protein boosts the immune system and the live active cultures promote a healthy gut. Be careful to read the label; some yogurt is processed with sugar.

#1. Choice in Dairy & Protein ▶ Whey isolate protein: In our world today, whey is known as the perfect protein, a milk product that doesn't act like milk. It is most suited for smoothies or mixed into yogurt. It is an antioxidant and provides tremendous immune support. We recommend that you research it further and discover for yourself how it works best in your nutritional program.

Eggs

Eating 3-6 eggs per week supports great balanced health. Each egg contains only 77 calories, 5 grams of fat and 6 grams of protein with all 9 essential amino acids. Eggs are rich in iron, phosphorous, selenium and Vitamins A, B12, B2 and B5. Eggs have 113 mg. of choline, a very important nutrient for the brain. This antioxidant-loaded food also helps with eye diseases such as macular degeneration, cataracts, blood levels, and age-related eye disorders.

Eat omega-enriched or pasteurized eggs from free-range chickens. They have more nutrition than the eggs from factory-raised chickens. Cook the whole egg when possible; the yolks contain most of the nutrients. As a weight management tool, egg yolks helps to break down fat, fill you up and keep you full longer. In every way, eggs rank # 1 in weight control, blood sugar levels and health management. Egg whites offer essential amino acids necessary for optimum health

Eggs have a reputation for high cholesterol. The cholesterol found in eggs only turns to a bad cholesterol when paired with bread, potato and other grains. It not only digests to bad cholesterol, but also turns the starch to sugar.

Dairy Tips & Recommendations

- Do not overcook your eggs; overcooking decreases the nutrition. Soft-boiled or soft-scrambled eggs are a good idea.
- Eggs do not, in and of themselves, increase cholesterol. Although eggs have 212 mg of cholesterol, they will only increase the good cholesterol (HDL). Like all foods, this is only true when you stay true with proper food pairing. Eggs also help to convert the bad cholesterol, LDL, to good cholesterol.
- When eggs are eaten without the proper pairing, the combination of foods may create an increase in bad cholesterol. Always eat eggs (fat and protein) with other fats and proteins along with clean vegetables.
- Eliminate any starchy vegetables, grains, rice, or wheat ingredients and the egg will digest as a pure protein.

NOTES

Fats

Fish Oil is a primary source of Omega-3 fatty acids. These are found in oily fish such as salmon, mackerel, tuna, sardines and herring, as well as in green nuts and seeds. Fish oil is essential in the digestive system. It increases valuable compounds in fruits, vegetables and other foods as they are traveling through the intestines and bowels. It is also responsible for lowering the glycemic load (critical for diabetes, but necessary for all).

Flaxseed Oil promotes hormone and prostrate health and is superior in anti-aging effects and antioxidants. It's good for the digestive system, heart, skin, brain and as a hormone replacement therapy, reducing menopausal symptoms in women. Flaxseed is very high in essential fatty acids including Omega-3s, and protects against arthritis, cancer and cardiovascular disease. Flaxseed and flaxseed oil are superior in the prevention of hormone-related cancers such as breast, cervical, uterine and prostate cancer. Use cold pressed oil.

Extra Virgin Olive Oil lowers the bad LDL cholesterol and raises the good HDL cholesterol. It also helps with skin cancer, depression, mental health, osteoporosis, type 2 diabetes, rheumatoid arthritis, obesity, diabetes, blood pressure, oxidative stress, heart disease, cancer, and metabolic syndrome. It can help prevent colon and bowel cancer, heart disease, and arthritis.

Macadamia Oil Some people feel that macadamia oil might be even more beneficial than olive oil. It provides all the same valuable minerals, vitamins and health benefits as olive oil but is also higher in monounsaturated fats (Omega-9s). Macadamia oil also reduces chronic inflammation and cholesterol.

Coconut Oil Coconut oil promotes a healthy digestive system, helping get rid of bad bacteria and inflammation, and helps relieve stomach ulcers. This oil also works to combat gonorrhea, genital infections, and candida yeast infections – but it can also help increase sex hormones. Coconut oil is an antioxidant and helps in preventing cancer, epilepsy, Alzheimer's and heart disease. It has a neutral effect on blood and cholesterol. Coconut is considered a super food for brain function and a better saturated fat than dairy or red meat. It also helps with weight loss and helps to reduce belly fat. When you need to reduce your calorie intake in the evening, include coconut oil at lunch.

Almond Oil Almond oil helps reduce inflammation that leads to heart attacks, cancer, Alzheimer's and many other diseases. Almond oil has a lot of the same benefits as olive and macadamia but in lesser amounts; still, it is one of the top foods. Its available source of Vitamins E and K stays true (doesn't degrade) even when heated, which is better than other oils.

Almond Butter Almond oil found in almond butter lowers blood lipids (cholesterol), is high in fiber, minerals, magnesium, Vitamin B6 and E, and lowers the risk of heart disease and cancer.

Hemp Seed Oil This oil is rated the best in balanced fatty acids (Omegas -3,-6 and -9). It helps alleviate symptoms of pre-menstrual syndrome, and helps to lower blood pressure and bad cholesterol. The Omega fatty acids reduce inflammation and can help with depression and mood. Hemp is high in all Omega fatty acids, and is a source of protein, fiber, phosphorus, potassium, magnesium, sulfur and calcium. Use cold.

Peanut Butter and Oil These favorite foods reduce belly fat when eaten alone or with a non-starchy vegetable; they also lower cholesterol and reduce the appetite. Peanut butter and peanut oil are very high antioxidant agents as well as anti-cancer agents. They can help prevent heart disease. They are high in magnesium, folic acid, fiber, copper, Vitamin E, niacin, and Vitamin B. Peanut butter and peanut oil have positive effects on the digestive system as well as the skin, heart, nerves and cardiovascular system. They help to reduce chronic inflammation.

Sesame Oil Sesame oil lowers blood pressure, is a superb antioxidant, and supports a healthy heart. Sesame oil is rich in minerals, fiber, protein, iron, magnesium, copper, phosphorus and potassium. Use unrefined, cold pressed and organic. While this oil can be heated to lower temperatures, remember to keep it refrigerated when not in use.

Nuts and Seeds

Nuts contain about 80-120 calories with 2-5 grams of fiber in ¼-cup. Nuts are a healthy monounsaturated fat, and help reduce the risk of heart disease, PMS, osteoporosis, and high cholesterol. A good source of fiber, nuts also provide Vitamin E and potassium. See previous two pages about oils made from nuts for a complete list of health benefits.

PAW, (pecan, almond and walnuts) are the 3 major nuts. This combination is used in many *Canna* recipes:

> Almonds contain Omega-3s, Vitamin E, potassium, calcium phosphorus, and magnesium. Almonds assist in weight loss, control of diabetes and stabilization of blood sugar. These nuts also act as an antioxidant and can alleviate arthritis and inflammation.
>
> Walnuts and Pecans contain Omega-3s, Vitamin E, fiber, calcium, magnesium, phosphorus, manganese and potassium. They help alleviate the symptoms of PMS, diabetes, arthritis, and inflammation. These nuts lower blood pressure and cholesterol, promote a healthy heart, help maintain eye health and can reduce the risk of coronary artery disease. They may help increase memory, fight depression, act as a mood booster, and promote good feelings and clear thinking. Walnuts and pecans are used for weight loss and appetite control by replacing bad calories with good calories that are healthier and more filling.
>
> Peanuts (legume) Peanut kernels are high in Vitamins E and B-6, niacin, copper, manganese, potassium, calcium, iron, magnesium, zinc, and selenium. They are loaded with resveratrol, responsible for cancer prevention (especially stomach cancer), and promote heart and coronary health. These nuts contribute to weight loss and help combat degenerative nerve disease, Alzheimer's, and infections.
>
> Pistachios These nuts are packed with potassium, Vitamins K and B-6, fiber, thiamine, phosphorus and magnesium. They promote good cholesterol and reduce bad cholesterol; promote healthy heart and veins, support prostrate health, and can assist in weight loss. For lunch try 1 ounce of pistachios, enjoy them slowly to savor their great flavor and finish with a tall glass of water. This just might lesson your appetite later in the day while giving you that healthy but yummy salty crunchy fix.

Seeds

Chia and flax seeds These seeds are very high in Omega-3s, but they are not a replacement for fish oil. Unless you are vegetarian or vegan, include fish in your diet for the best and most complete source of Omega-3s. Chia and flax seeds are rich in antioxidants and fiber, magnesium, zinc, iron and calcium.

Pumpkin seeds These contain heart-healthy magnesium, potassium, manganese, copper, protein, zinc and Vitamin B6. Pumpkin seeds help to lower cholesterol, build strong bones and teeth, provide immune support, and support a healthy gut and bowel function. They help with sleep and mood; enhance the senses of taste, smell, and vision; improve skin strength, and help improve male sexual function.

Fats Tips and Recommendations
Never reuse your cooking oils. When a fat has been heated, especially for a long period of time, the benefits are not only diminished but the oil could degrade and turn rancid. At Love Buds, our *Canna* Fats are heated just enough to expose the cannabis properties but not high enough to spoil the fat.

Fruits

Eat fruit on an empty stomach, or wait 1-2 hours between eating fruit and other foods

Berries

Blackberries 65 calories and 2 grams of fiber in ½ cup. Blackberries contain Vitamin A, and are helpful in fighting inflammation.

Blueberries 85 calories and 4 grams of fiber in 1 cup. Loaded in fiber, Vitamins C and K and manganese, blueberries are a healthy antioxidant and help in preventing cancer. They also work to alleviate symptoms of diabetes, Alzheimer's, Parkinson's disease, the nervous system, heart disease, and arthritis. They promote a clear mind and memory, and help strengthen the urinary tract and eye health.

Raspberries 65 calories and 8 grams of fiber in 1 cup. Raspberries contain calcium, magnesium, phosphorus, potassium, and Vitamins C and K. They help fight cancer, are antiviral and antibacterial. Raspberries can help reduce pain and inflammation from arthritis, and are an antioxidant and memory enhancer.

Strawberries 50 calories and 3 grams of fiber in 1 cup. Along with the other benefits of berries, strawberries dipped in dark chocolate boost serotonin and endorphin levels, so there are real health benefits to this favorite treat!

Other fruits

Cherries 75 calories and 2 grams of fiber in 1 cup. Cherries are a kind of super food. In any shape or form, they are effective in relieving arthritis and gout. Anti-inflammatory, antiviral and antibacterial, they contain the same resveratrol found in red wine. Cherries help fight cancer, heart disease and stroke. Eating tart cherries can help with sleep, restlessness and anxiety.

Kiwi fruit 45 calories and 2 grams fiber in 1 kiwi. Kiwis contain more Vitamin C than any other fruit. They help fight cancer and heart disease, are an antioxidant, and are high in healthy enzymes. Some people use Kiwi fruit daily as a blood thinner in place of aspirin.

Avocado 200 calories and 15 grams of fiber in 1 cup. Known as one of the "good fats," avocados are an antioxidant and are anti-inflammatory; they contain potassium, folic acid, Vitamin A and beta carotene. They help reduce joint and muscle pain, and reduce the risk of heart disease, cancer, and diabetes. Avocados reduce the bad cholesterol (LDL) and increase the good cholesterol (HDL). They help with weight loss as well as eye, heart, and skin health. Try to include avocados in your diet 3-5 times each week.

Cantaloupe See Melons

Coconut 100-200 calories and 4 grams of fiber in 1 cup. Coconut and coconut oil are among the healthiest fats there are; they support our entire system. Coconut helps support cardiovascular health, kidneys, and a healthy digestive system and colon. It works as an anti-cancer agent, and helps to stabilize the immune system, cholesterol levels, and hormone levels.

Guava 45 calories and 5 grams of fiber in 1 fruit. Guava contains Vitamins C and A, folic acid, calcium, magnesium, potassium and beta-carotene. It serves as an antioxidant and promotes artery health, immune strength, nervous system strength and joint health. Guava fruit helps to fight cancer, heart disease, stroke, high blood pressure, arthritis, pain and inflammation. They help control diabetes and obesity, and aid in weight loss.

Apples 60-80 calories and 5 grams fiber in 1 medium apple. Apples contain Vitamin A and minerals, and protect against cancers including prostrate, liver, colon and lung cancer. A powerful antioxidant, apples repress tumors and promote cardiovascular health, and help with osteoporosis, asthma, diabetes and weight issues.

Apricots 45 calories in 3 fresh apricots; 80 calories and 1 gram of fiber in ¼-cup of dried apricots. Apricots contain Vitamin A, beta-carotene and potassium. They reduce the risk of lung and colon cancer and arthritis. Dried apricots are higher in calories but are still very healthy in small amounts.

Bananas 100 calories and 4 grams of fiber in 1 banana. Bananas contain potassium and Vitamin A, and the inner peel is high in nutrition. Bananas help settle an upset stomach, providing it with good bacteria. They also help strengthen the immune system, regulate fluids, help with hypertension, and can reduce the risk of kidney cancer.

Cranberries 20 calories in ½ cup raw cranberries; 30 calories in ⅓-cup of dried, sweetened cranberries. Cranberries contain fiber, Vitamin K, and are a strong antioxidant. They support healthy teeth and gums, ward off urinary tract infections and help with pelvic issues, stomach lining problems and ulcers. They can also reduce cramps and lower the risk of several cancers.

Dates 65 calories and 1 gram of fiber per date. Dates contain calcium, magnesium, potassium and Vitamin A, and are a leading antioxidant. Because of their high sugar content, they are not recommended for diabetics, those with high blood sugar, or general weight loss.

Figs 20 calories and 1 gram of fiber per fig. Figs are high in calcium and potassium, and help out with heart disease, stroke and blood pressure.

Gogi berries 90 calories and 4 grams of fiber in ¼ cup. Gogi berries are an antioxidant, and support the immune system. They have been known to aid in sexual stamina and potency.

Grapefruit 120 calories and 2 grams of fiber in 1 grapefruit. Red grapefruit is preferable. Grapefruit contains potassium and Vitamins C and A. As an antioxidant, it also helps to reduce pain and Inflammation, and fights various cancers. Avoid grapefruit if you are prone to kidney stones. The low-calorie, high water content helps with weight loss and cholesterol.

Grapes 95 calories and 1 gram of fiber for 1 cup dark grapes. Grapes contain Vitamins C, K and A, and potassium. Dark grapes have high levels of resveratrol, are an antioxidant, and reduce the risk of cardiovascular disease and cancer. Grapes lower the bad LDL cholesterol while raising the good HDL cholesterol and are known as a life extender.

Lemons and Limes 15 calories and 4 grams of fiber in 1 fruit. Lemons and limes are high in Vitamin C. They are antioxidants; reduce pain and inflammation; promote liver and kidney health, and are often used as a detox when combined with hot water, maple syrup and cayenne pepper. They reduce kidney stones, cholesterol and the risk of several cancers.

Mangos 99 calories and 3 grams of fiber in one cup of mangos. Mangos contain potassium, Vitamins C and K, calcium, phosphorus and magnesium. Although the sugar content is high, the glycemic load in a small-to-medium-size mango is only 7, safe for most diabetic and low-sugar diets.

Melons Melons contain potassium, magnesium, Vitamin C and lots of water.

Honeydew melons have a strong role in weight management, and help to reduce heart disease, blood pressure and strokes.

Cantaloupes 100 calories and 1 gram of fiber in ½-melon. Cantaloupes contain potassium, beta-carotene, Vitamin A, calcium and magnesium. They help fight heart disease, stroke, high blood pressure, and cancer, and strengthen the immune system. The low calories, water volume and great taste make cantaloupe a good food for weight loss.

Watermelon 50 calories and 1 gram of fiber per cup. Called the "happy fruit," watermelon provides sensual endorphins, can have Viagra-like effects, and lessens depression. As with all melons, watermelon is a great fruit for weight loss and managing diabetes due to its low glycemic load. Watermelon is loaded with compounds for bone strength, and reduces the risk of rheumatoid arthritis and several types of cancer.

Oranges 60 calories and 3 grams of fiber in 1 fruit. This category includes tangerines and nectarines. Oranges contain Vitamin C, are antioxidant, and help to protect against aging and several types of cancer. They are antiviral, antifungal and anti-bacterial. This amazing fruit lowers cholesterol, is anti-inflammatory, strengthens capillaries, lowers blood pressure, protects the heart and fights infections. Because most store-bought orange juice contains sugar, try eating a chilled orange or squeeze the juice from oranges yourself.

Papaya 60 calories and 5 grams of fiber in 1 cup. Papaya contains potassium, calcium, Vitamins C and A, beta-carotene, and digestive enzymes. It serves as an antioxidant and is anti-inflammatory; helps fight pain and the symptoms of arthritis, and helps to keep the immune system and eyes strong. Papaya reduces the risk of lung and colon cancer, rheumatoid arthritis and stomach ulcers, and fights aging.

Peaches 40-60 calories and 2 grams of fiber in 1 fruit. Peaches are anti-inflammatory, antioxidant and anti-aging. They support skin cell growth and a strong immune system, and have a low impact on blood sugar levels.

Pineapple 65-75 calories and 2 grams of fiber per cup. Pineapples contain magnesium, Vitamin C and potassium, assist with digestive enzymes and lower blood sugar. They are anti-inflammatory and have been known to reduce pain, manage arthritis, thin the blood, and fight cancer and tumors.

Plums 70 calories and 2 grams of fiber in 3 fruits. Plums contain resveratrol and Vitamin C, and serve as an antioxidant. They fight aging as well.

Prunes 100 calories and 3 grams of fiber per fresh prune; 200 calories for dried prunes. Prunes are considered a super power in antioxidants. They contain fiber, potassium, Vitamin C and iron. Prunes support a healthy gut and are known for cleaning out the digestive system and colon. They reduce the risk of colon and breast cancer, diverticular disease, heart and cardiovascular disease, and diabetes. Prunes are a good addition for weight loss as a dessert loaded with fiber.

Pears 100 calories and 5 grams of fiber in 1 fruit. Pears contain potassium, calcium and phosphorus, and are known to support eye health.

Pomegranate 70 calories and 1 gram of fiber in 1 fruit. Known in ancient mythology as the love fruit, pomegranates are antioxidants and anti-inflammatory, and help reduce plaque in arteries. Pomegranate seeds and fiber are great in juice, smoothies and cocktails.

Quince 50 calories and 2 grams fiber in 1 fruit. This fruit is high in pectin, potassium and Vitamin C, and makes a great addition to winter cooking.

Star fruit 30 calories and 4 grams of fiber in 1 fruit. Star fruit contains Vitamin C and potassium, helps to clear up diarrhea.

Fruit Tips & Recommendations
Experiment with eating or juicing with the skins on for a greater dose of everything.

NOTES

Grains and Rice

If you have problems with gluten intolerance, diabetes, celiac disease, gout or kidney stones, be very careful that you pair grains and rice with the proper foods.

Brewer's yeast
"Brewer's yeast itself isn't found in nature. It's made domestically from a single-celled fungus or yeast called Saccharomyces cerevisiae that is ground and dried… Brewer's yeast is either grown for harvest on grains, hops, sugar beets or molasses, or it's what's left over after beer has been brewed and processed… Brewer's yeast has been available as a nutritional supplement for many years"
See http://bit.ly/1LTRQUI.

Brewer's yeast helps to break down carbohydrates and fats for energy. It can reduce cholesterol, blood sugar, and some forms of cancer. Brewer's yeast has been found to prevent DNA damage and improve immune function. A super star in helping to reduce the spread of Salmonella and E-coli, Brewer's yeast is high in low-fat protein, B Vitamins, and minerals selenium and chromium.

Brown Rice
180 calories and 2 grams fiber for ¼-cup uncooked rice. Brown rice contains niacin, Vitamin B6, phosphorus and magnesium. It's a great substitute for other types of carbs, and will help fight heart disease, high cholesterol, and cancer. One caution: brown rice has a high glycemic impact.

Oatmeal
Old fashioned, thick rolled or steel-cut oats – 140 calories and 5 grams fiber in 1 cup. An antioxidant, oatmeal contains protein, provides immune system support, lowers cholesterol, and stabilizes blood sugar.

Quinoa
150 calories and 3 grams fiber in ¼-cup, uncooked. Quinoa, which is gluten-free, contains Vitamins B and E, iron, calcium, phosphorus, magnesium, potassium, copper, manganese and zinc. It helps to battle cancer and anemia, and build strong bones.

Breads

Whole Wheat Bread 120-150 calories and 3-5 grams of fiber in 1 slice. Whole wheat bread contains calcium, magnesium, potassium, folic acid, and Vitamins B6, E and K.

Grain Tips & Recommendations

- Choose whole grains like cracked wheat, buckwheat, sprouted wheat, spelt, or rye. Our favorite is Ezekiel, found in the freezer section of any health food store.
- Replace ½ of the flour with wheat germ for greater benefits.
- Use only the grains listed in our Love Buds guide. Grains can be especially tricky; if not paired properly, wheat can cause an insulin spike and sugar conversion.
- For optimum conversion in the digestive system, pair grains, starches and rice with vegetables only, without the presence of fat, protein or fruit. When starches are paired with nonfat dairy and or vegetables the starch digests as healthy fuel. When starches and grains are combined with protein, fats, fruits, or fatty dairy, the starch digests as sugar, turning to a bad fat. That type of fat can cause higher sugar levels, raise cholesterol and blood pressure, and stores as belly fat. Enjoy starches with nonfat dairy like skim milk, and pasta with oil free marinara sauce. Soups and dishes made with vegetables and fat-free vegetable broth are always a good choice.
- Be careful with pasta: eat pasta with vegetables **only**. When you combine anything other than vegetables, pasta turns to sugar and disrupts the entire system.
- Breads should be coupled with veggies without the presence of fat or protein.
- Wrap protein in leafy greens or egg tortillas without the presence of starch.
- When cooking with grains and rice, consider using tea in place of water for an extra antioxidant boost.

Legumes and Beans

Beans and legumes share many of the same benefits, with just 50-100 calories and 10-18 grams of fiber in one cup. They are high in antioxidants, vitamins and minerals, including folic acid, iron, zinc, magnesium, and potassium, and offer essential amino acids for optimum health. Beans are a great protein for those not eating meat. Legumes and beans in general help to lower the risk of breast, colon, prostrate and other cancers, as well as lower cholesterol and fight heart disease. They can help to control diabetes and weight gain, and stabilize blood pressure and blood sugars. Kidney, mung and lentils are more beneficial for the reproductive system than other types of legumes and are much easier to digest.

- Some research findings suggest that soy might not be a good food source for rheumatoid arthritis and other autoimmune diseases.
- Pairing foods high in Vitamin C like tomatoes or peppers with a non-meat source like beans, black beans and tofu helps your body take in iron.

Listed in importance of vitamins, minerals, fiber and calories:
- Kidney Beans and Lentils
- Mung beans, Pinto and Red Beans
- Black Beans, Chickpeas, Garbanzo beans
- Peas: green peas are actually lentils
- Navy Beans

Soy

Soy beans: We have added soy (tofu) to our list for those having issues with other protein foods. Among the soy list our favorites are edamame (green soybeans) for snacks, with miso and tempeh for recipes.

Miso and Tempeh (fermented soybeans): These may help with symptoms of menopause. Combine miso with vegetables to balance the high sodium. Tempeh tastes and acts like mushrooms. Soy products can help prevent prostate enlargement and may slow tumor growth.

Legumes & Beans Tips & Recommendations

For vegan and low-fat recipes, beans and legumes rank at the top of the list.
- Eating beans and legumes 3-to-4 times per week is especially valuable for those prone to diabetes and obesity. Replacing most red meat with beans is an extraordinarily healthful choice. Those who suffer with gas from the consumption of beans could choose lentils, including green peas.

NOTES

Protein (Meat and Fish)

Proteins are listed in order of highest benefits and/or lowest calories. Each serving should be equal to the size of your palm, or a little larger if you are highly active and athletic. Fatty fish, meats and poultry contain approximately 100-200 calories per 4-ounce serving, but keep in mind that the fattier proteins have a higher level of healthy Omega fatty acids.

> Wild game 170 calories in 4 ounces. Venison, buffalo and other wild game are lean meats, low in fat but with great taste.
>
> Poultry 175-250 calories in 4 ounces. Poultry offers essential amino acids necessary for good health. Includes chicken, turkey and Cornish game hens.
>
> Lamb 190 calories in 4 ounces. Lamb contains iron and zinc, and is a good protein for those with allergies.
>
> Fish 170-250 calories in 4 ounces. Fish are a primary source of Omega-3 fatty acids and an excellent source of protein. Canned fish with bones is usually much higher in health benefits, providing a good dose of calcium.
>
> Beef 200-250 calories in 4 ounces of lean meat. Loaded with beneficial iron, vitamin B12 and protein.
>
> Liver 200 calories in 4 ounces. Healthy grass fed cows liver is loaded with a wide spectrum on vitamins, minerals, protein and fat.

Fresh-Water Fish & Seafood

Fish and seafood contribute to brain development in the fetus, and provide essential amino acids necessary for optimum health. Canned, fresh or frozen versions of these foods are included here. There can be less than 100 calories for raw fish; the calorie count rises depending upon how it's cooked. The following calorie counts are estimates only.

First choice in fish and seafood:

Salmon 200 calories in 4 ounces of fresh salmon. Salmon (including canned salmon), is high in Omega-3s and helps with chronic inflammation and circulation. Salmon is great for a healthy heart, beautiful skin, healthy brain cells, and a stronger memory.

Sardines 25 calories in 1 sardine. Sardines are high in Omega-3s. Be sure you purchase sardines canned in sardine oil only -- not any other kind of oil. Don't purchase sardines fresh-frozen. Canned sardines are one of the best sources of Omega-3s without the risk of heavy metals.

Mackerel 200 calories in 4 ounces. These fish are also high in Omega-3s. Mackerel from the Atlantic has a smoother flavor; from the Pacific, a stronger flavor. Prepare mackerel as you would tuna, trout and salmon; similar in flavor, health benefits and texture, mackerel has a stronger taste and smell.

Second choice in fish and seafood: Calories range between 100 for fresh fish and about 300 for cooked fish for 4 ounces. The following fish offer similar health benefits as listed above only with fewer Omega-3s.

Mahi-Mahi, Swordfish, Tilapia and Tuna (Bluefin tuna rates higher in health benefits)

Catfish, Cod, Flounder, Grouper, Haddock, Halibut, Orange Roughy, Pollack and Wild Herring

Shellfish: Includes Clams, Crab, Mussels, Oysters, Scallops & Shrimp 100-130 calories in 4 ounces. Shrimp and crab have the highest calorie content. Shellfish contain Omega-3s, minerals, Iron, zinc and copper.

Spices

Black Pepper antioxidant, anti-inflammatory and anti-flatulence black pepper helps fight cancer and diabetes, improves digestion (and increases digestion enzymes). It improves taste buds, heart rate and blood pressure, sooths indigestion and relieves nausea.

Chlorella powder antioxidant, contains fiber, Vitamins C and A, and minerals. A detoxifying agent, chlorella powder helps fight cancer and high cholesterol; aids in digestion and immune support and provides the same benefits as super greens.

Cilantro Also known as Chinese parsley, cilantro is an antioxidant. It contains Vitamins A, C and K; improves appetite and digestion; aids with vision, heart rate and blood pressure; and helps fight cancer.

Cinnamon Cinnamon relieves gas, aids digestion, kills bad bacteria, helps pelvic issues, relieves cramps, is an appetite stimulant. Helps to control diabetes, fights pain inflammation, promotes joint health, and works to strengthen the immune system; reduces blood sugar and bad cholesterol.

Garlic This antioxidant is known as "nature's healer;" in its raw form, garlic is a potent antibiotic. It helps lower blood pressure and cholesterol, prevents blood clots, pain and inflammation, and helps to control diabetes. Garlic intensifies cancer-fighting compounds. Smash garlic and let it sit for 10 minutes to release the flavors and aromas.

Ginger An antioxidant, ginger lowers cholesterol, relieves the pain and inflammation of fibromyalgia and arthritis, and improves circulation. It helps relieve morning sickness, sea sickness and general nausea. Aids the stomach and digestion, and has a blood thinning effect. Ginger is an aid with men's and women's health.

Green Power Powder This powder is high in antioxidants, contains trace minerals and vitamins, increases stamina, weight loss, mental clarity, and energy. Normally used as a juice which is 100 percent absorbable, it is vegetarian, caffeine-free, fat-free, and low in carbohydrates. *Love buds Green Power Powder* contains barley grass, wheat grass, spirulina, spinach, alfalfa leaf, kelp, dulse leaf (red algae), orange peel, barley grass juice, beet root, dandelion leaf, lemon peel, ginkgo leaf and wheat grass juice.

Oregano anti-inflammatory, antioxidant, anti-bacterial, anti-fungal; promotes brain and joint health. Oregano aids in good digestion and supports the immune system. Help's with men's and women's issues, relieves candida infections, and is known to be a sexual stimulant.

Rosemary anti-inflammatory, helps relieve symptoms of Alzheimer's, and asthma; provides support for men's and women's issues, memory and sharpness of the mind and heart; supports the liver.

Sage anti-inflammatory, antioxidant, anti-viral, antibiotic; supports brain health, helps control diabetes. Sage helps with men's issues and with women's issues such as candida and night sweats; helps ease rheumatoid arthritis, pain and inflammation; lowers blood pressure. Caution: avoid sage preparation during pregnancy and while breastfeeding.

Saffron antioxidant and anti-inflammatory, saffron promotes health in many ways. It helps fight depression and aging, relives insomnia, gas, indigestion and stomach aches. Saffron helps relieve symptoms of asthma, slows the heart rate, and lowers blood pressure as well as cholesterol and triglycerides. It helps with brain health, memory and recall, and age-related mental impairments. Saffron has a good effect on sexual hormones and can help increase men's endurance. It provides support to the nervous system and helps relieve neurodegenerative disorders. Due to its incredible taste, healing and health benefits, saffron is a super spice. However, it's very expensive. They say saffron costs more than gold and it's no wonder. The labor-intensive harvest, seasonal growing limits and import cost keep this spice very expensive. It takes about 80,000 crocus flowers to produce 1 pound of saffron threads. Read about the incredible benefits of saffron here: http://wb.md/1mqDezM.

Tips & Recommendations:
- Soak saffron threads in a hot liquid, preferably milk, for 15 minutes. Add to grains, rice, quinoa, soups and stew. Saffron tea is used to manage psoriasis; saffron broth helps to stimulate digestion. Drink saffron water daily for mind and body wellness: mix ½ -1 gm saffron to 1 liter water.
- Spices, when heated, release their full aroma, flavors & healing benefits.

Eat any time you like:

Apple Pie Spice Cinnamon, ginger, allspice, clove and nutmeg (see individual spices for health benefits)

Allspice Cinnamon, clove and nutmeg (see individual spices for health benefits)

Basil Anti-depressant, anti-fungal, antioxidant, anti-spasmodic; helps with diabetes, cancer, colds, headaches, heart disease and stomach disorders.

Cardamom Aphrodisiac, antioxidant, anti-inflammatory; used as a detox and a diuretic; helps with diabetes, digestion (eases stomach cramps and reduces gas), and depression. Cardamom promotes oral health and fresh breath, fights colds and cancer; helps lower blood pressure and strengthen the liver. Caution: do not use if you have gallstones; ask your physician.

Chili Powder Antioxidant, contains Vitamins A and C and minerals. Relives symptoms of arthritis, pain and inflammation, helps fight cancer, improves the immune system; known to be a sexual stimulant.

Chives Antioxidant, supports brain health, helps control diabetes, good for women's and men's issues.

Chocolate (dark) Antioxidant, helps lower blood pressure and cholesterol, helps fight cardiovascular disease and diabetes; is a subtle aphrodisiac.

Cloves Antioxidant, anti-fungal, anti-bacterial, anti-inflammatory, antiseptic; help strengthen bones, fights diabetes; is good for gum health, and the intestines. Cloves contain Omega-3s, vitamins and minerals.

Cocoa Antioxidant; helps promote a healthy heart, boosts the mood and spirit, and is known to create a romantic atmosphere.

Cumin Antioxidant; helps relieve asthma, diabetes, and heartburn; helps with immunity, insomnia, digestive and respiratory health, and fights cancer.

Fennel Helps relieve digestive problems including constipation, diarrhea, indigestion, and flatulence. Fennel relieves colic, inflammation, respiratory disorders, and menstrual disorders. It promotes eye health.

Flax Omega-3s and fiber; helps with cardiovascular and colon health, immunity, blood sugar balance and healthy skin. Flax relieves menopausal symptoms; helps fight cancer.

Ginkgo Biloba An anti-aging nutritional supplement that helps reduce anxiety, depression and seasonal effective disorder; helps relieve symptoms of asthma, diabetes, PMS, migraines, schizophrenia, thyroid disorder, ADHD, multiple sclerosis and vertigo. Ginkgo Biloba helps with circulation, blood pressure, brain health, cancer prevention and care, eye disease, memory improvement, women's health, kidney care, erectile dysfunction, and mood.

Gravel Root Helps with women's issues, kidney stones, urinary track, rheumatism and gout.

Horseradish An antioxidant and anti-inflammatory, horseradish is high in Vitamin C, fiber, potassium and minerals. It increases appetite and aids in digestion, helps to detoxify and acts as a liver cleanse. It aids in tumor and cancer prevention and helps to boost the immunity.

Licorice (black) Soothes the throat and lungs, stimulates digestion and helps relieve indigestion. Aids as an anti-cancer treat and supports women's issues, especially menopause. Soothes the joints and helps to balance blood sugar.

Marjoram Anti-bacterial, anti-viral, antioxidant, and anti-inflammatory spice, marjoram contains Vitamins C, A and K and minerals. It aids in digestion, helps build the immune system, fights Alzheimer's and age-related eye health and sleep disorders.

Mustard Seed An aphrodisiac, mustard seed protects against tumor growth, stimulates the appetite, aids in circulation and serves as a detox.

Olives In brine, water, or salted in virgin oil, olives promote gastrointestinal health, boost the immune system, aids in men's issues, relieve pain and inflammation and serve as a sexual stimulant.

Orange Peel Anti-aging, antioxidant, and anti-inflammatory, orange peels help fight Alzheimer's, and boost brain health and memory.

Parsley An antioxidant, parsley contains Vitamins A and C, iron and copper. It promotes brain and eye health, and builds strong bones. Aids in blood pressure, diabetes, cancer, kidney health, and weight loss. Helps relieve pain and inflammation and freshens the breath.

Peppermint Soothes the stomach and helps to relieve indigestion and curb cravings; help relieve nervousness and irritability and reduces tension headaches; boosts concentration.

Periwinkle An anti-aging flower and herb, periwinkle promotes brain health, concentration and memory. Fights Alzheimer's, strengthens the immune system, and helps relieve diarrhea.

Red Clover Aids in a number of conditions, including cancer, women's issues, menopause, osteoporosis, fluid retention, bladder health, urology, men's health, whooping cough, respiratory problems, circulation and cardiovascular health. Helps as a liver cleanse.

Sea Salt Contains essential minerals, salt is essential for life and a healthy heart, and for retaining much-needed hydration.

Thyme Antioxidant, antiseptic, anti-fungal, this herb is high in vitamins and minerals. It promotes brain health, helps to control diabetes, assists with digestion, and reduces stress. Thyme is also good for regulating heart rate and blood pressure.

Turmeric Good for the colon, liver and urinary tract; a detoxifying agent; alleviates arthritis pain and inflammation; helps with women's issues and PMS; helps to lower cholesterol.

Wasabi Anti-inflammatory and antioxidant, wasabi contains fiber, minerals, potassium, and Vitamin C. It helps to relieve arthritis, pain and inflammation; increases appetite and aids in digestion; boosts immunity and helps with tumor prevention. Wasabi also acts to fight cancer and is a detoxifying agent.

Raw Apple Cider Vinegar Antibiotic, and antiseptic, raw apple cider vinegar contains potassium, phosphorous, minerals, pectin, malic acid, calcium, ash, and acetic acid. It boosts digestion, promotes a healthy bowel, reduces toxins, alleviates joint pain and stiffness, clears skin breakouts, and helps with weight loss. It also breaks down fat for fuel, alleviates symptoms of osteoarthritis and arthritis, and helps to regulate blood sugar. Caution: do not cook in aluminum, copper or cast iron; add vinegar after you remove from the heat. Vinegar and honey help to dissolve calcium deposits.

For a complete list of healthy, healing *Canna Spice* Blends, see Ch.1, pgs.21-23

Sweeteners

Best choices:

Bee Pollen Propolis 42 calories in 1 tablespoon. Bee pollen fights infections, and contains 18 amino acids, digestive enzymes, Vitamins A, B1, B2, B6, B12 and niacin. Kills colon cancer cells and boosts prostate cancer cell death. Treats allergies, bone disease, lowers blood pressure and kills bacteria.

Honey 64 calories in 1 tablespoon. Use the raw, unfiltered honey found in health food stores; is an antioxidant. If you react to honey, use stevia. Honey is a natural sugar.

Black Strap Molasses 47 calories in 1 tablespoon. Unsulfured molasses is low in sugar and high in nutrients including iron, potassium, calcium, magnesium and copper.

Use the following as you like, but beware of the sugar, including natural sweeteners.

Dark chocolate 170 calories in 1 tablespoon. Be sure it's 70% cocoa or greater; contains magnesium and nitric oxide; lowers the risk of cardiovascular disease, lowers blood pressure and blood sugar (sugar free chocolate). Chocolate might create inflammation in some women.

Jelly (sugar free) 10 calories in 1 tablespoon. See *Canna* Spiced Jelly in Ch.10, pgs. 272-275.

Dates 140 calories and 4 grams of fiber in 6 dates. The fruit is rich in dietary fiber, which prevents LDL cholesterol absorption in the gut. Dates increase energy, and are excellent sources of iron and potassium, and are a valuable antioxidant.

Figs 4 figs contain 125 calories and 5 grams fiber. For a rich textured sweetener, blend ¼-cup water with 1 fig. Figs are naturally rich in phytonutrients and anti-oxidants. Dried figs are highly concentrated source of minerals and vitamins.

Licorice 140 calories in 2 vines of black licorice. Licorice soothes the throat and lungs, stimulates digestion and alleviates indigestion, and is an anti-cancer agent. Licorice supports women's issues, especially menopause; it also soothes joints and normalizes blood sugar.

Maple Syrup: 52 calories in 1 tablespoon. Pure maple syrup is an anti-aging and antioxidant agent; it fights cancer, is an immune booster and soothes the stomach. Loaded with vitamins and minerals, it is a natural sugar.

Golden Raisins: 2 calories in 1 raisin. Raisins are an antioxidant and anti-inflammatory; they improve brain function, fight cancer, are a source of fiber, aids in digestion and a healthy heart.

Rose buds and petals: They calm, detoxify, help with hydration, are anti-bacterial and anti-inflammatory, and are high in Vitamin C. They can be used as a subtle sweetener or gentle flavor.

Sugar Substitutes

Keep an open mind and stay current with all the latest information as to the real benefits of food substitutes.

Stevia: 0 calories, no value, some fiber
Xylitol: 0 calories, no value

Sweetener Tips & Recommendations

Breaking away from sugar and sweetened foods is one of the most difficult tasks there is. Studies have compared having a sweet tooth to an addiction; there is always the temptation to go back, and once back on sugar, it's that much harder to stay away. Keep in mind that sugar, is like poison for your body, particularly for your immune system. After you have been off sugar and heavy sweeteners long enough, you'll find your food begins to taste much better. You'll discover flavors you had been missing before. The sweeteners listed here are to help you break away from sugar while still giving you options for healthy meals and beverages.

Avoiding white, processed sugar is highly recommended; white sugar is never a good idea when your goal is to optimize your good health. Every summer during Oregon's berry season we make homemade jam, jelly and other preserves. Occasionally we make an exception and add a small amount of raw sugar, honey or maple syrup, along with non-sugar sweeteners like xylitol or stevia. However, these are seasonal exceptions.

NOTES

Vegetables

The top super stars. Enjoy daily!

Super Greens 35 calories and 3 to 4 grams of fiber in 1 cup. Super greens are a select group of dark, leafy green vegetables that offer more vitamins, minerals and fiber than any other food group (though some are not in the dark, leafy-green category). They're loaded with superior body and mind building blocks, and might be the best health food available. The number #1 super food is kimchi, which has added enzymes for the formation of flora, resulting in a healthy gut.

Dandelion Greens and Root Try to include this natural probiotic in your diet often, cooked or with other salad greens. Dandelions act as a urinary stimulant and are a natural diuretic. They also help detoxify the liver and gall bladder, help treat diabetes, stimulate digestion and release bile. They help with indigestion, hepatitis, emotional wellness, depression and mood swings. Dandelions support eye health and lower blood pressure.

Dandelion Root Extract and Greens These are super foods for diabetes; they help reduce high blood pressure; alleviates symptom of PMS and menopause, and assist with relieving water retention. They create stronger bile for digestion, relieve constipation, promote a healthy gut, and reduce heart burn and indigestion.

Kale Leading super vegetable, kale belongs to the cabbage family. It fights against breast, cervical and colon cancers; is anti-aging and an antioxidant. It's used to detoxify, fights free radicals, helps prevent macular degeneration, and DNA degradation. Kale is loaded with calcium, iron, and Vitamin A, C and K and contains 7 times the beta-carotene of broccoli. Supports weight control. Use the young soft leaves for salad and the larger older leaves for cooking. Flat leaves taste milder; curly leaves are a bit stronger.

Spinach The second leading super vegetable, spinach, contains Vitamins C and K, and calcium; it has more potassium than bananas. Spinach is excellent for cardiovascular, prostrate and brain health. It helps prevent muscular degeneration, helps lower cholesterol levels. spinach is one of the vegetables most contaminated with pesticides, so buy organic and wash well.

Swiss Chard A rich source of Vitamins C, A, K, and the B-complex, as well as beta-carotene, calcium, and potassium. Chard helps prevent osteoporosis, iron deficiency anemia, and vitamin A deficiency. It may help protect against cardiovascular diseases, colon and prostate cancers, and protect against macular degeneration. Do not overcook to keep the nutritional value.

Turnip Greens See turnips and super greens

Watercress Watercress is one of the great super foods related to the broccoli, kale and cabbage family. With only 4 calories, it has 4 times the calcium, magnesium, Vitamin C and iron than milk. Add daily to anything; it's light, loaded with minerals and vitamins, and very tasty. It supports the Immune system and helps prevent esophageal and gastrointestinal cancer.

Kimchi and Sauerkraut Buy fresh, not canned. 30 calories in 1 ounce. Kimchi consists of fermented cabbage and spices; sauerkraut consists of fermented cabbage and salt. These are both considered super foods, providing far more probiotics than any other food or supplement. Antioxidants, they provide immune support, help combat heart disease, breast cancer, and degenerative disease, and increases good cholesterol.

Sea Vegetables 11 calories in 1 tablespoon. A super food. Sea vegetables, or dried seaweed, contain essential vitamins and minerals, calcium, iodine, iron and protein. Good for wraps, snacks and flavoring. Sea vegetables provide 10 times the minerals of broccoli. They reduce inflammation and swelling, protect against environmental pollutants, and lower the risk of cancer.

Second Top Super Stars. Eat 3-5 times per week.

Beets and Greens 55 calories and 3 grams of fiber in one medium beet. Beets greens are exceptionally high in nutrients. Beets are a liver and blood cleanser, fight cancer, replenish iron from blood loss, help develop a healthy heart, and alleviate symptoms of stroke, dementia and vascular disease.

Broccoli 30 calories and 9 grams of fiber in 1 cup. Broccoli fights many forms of cancer. Its anti-aging, anti-antioxidant and detoxifying properties are valued by people who want to look younger and remain healthy. Helps prevent macular degeneration and blindness. High in potassium, calcium, folic acid, magnesium, phosphorus, beta-carotene and Vitamins C and A. Lightly cooked or blanched, broccoli is easier for the body to digest and releases vitamins, minerals and beta carotene. Broccoli is also used for weight control. Use the entire stalk, leaves and flower.

Broccoli Rabe 9 calories in 1 cup. Known as Chinese flowering cabbage, broccoli rabe is a cross between broccoli and turnip greens. It holds the same great rewards as broccoli and turnips, but is milder in flavor.

Brussels Sprouts 38 calories and 4 grams of fiber in 1 cup. "Mon petite chou," or "my little cabbage," Brussel sprouts can reduce the risk of colon, prostate and all other cancers. Should be included in weight management, and bone strengthening programs; high in vitamins and minerals.

Cabbage (red & purple) 19 calories and 4 grams of fiber in 1 cup cooked cabbage. Cabbage is high in Vitamins C and K, beta-carotene, calcium, magnesium and potassium. Fights breast, prostate and other cancers. A strong antioxidant, detoxifier and anti-inflammatory agent, it helps fight heart disease, strengthens connective tissue, promotes eye health and strong blood vessels.

Carrots 25 calories and almost 2 grams of fiber in 1 medium carrot. A super food, carrots fight many types of cancer. This antioxidant agent can improve eye health. Slightly cooked, carrots will give a higher nutritional release.

Celery 30 calories and 3 grams of fiber in 3 stalks. Celery helps lower blood pressure, the concentration of stress hormones and improves bone health. Fresh or cooked, celery stimulates saliva to aid digestion and weight control and lessens carb cravings.

Collard Greens 50 calories and 5 grams of fiber in 1 cup. Collard greens are high in calcium, magnesium, phosphorus, potassium, Vitamins C, A and K, and beta-carotene. They support eye health. With a mild taste and heavy texture, they are great sautéed or steamed and used for a wrap.

Grass, Alfalfa, Barley and Wheat Grass
15 calories and 1 gram of fiber in 1 ounce of concentrate. Primarily used as a juice, these help purify the blood, provide immune support, energy, stamina, clear thinking and increase the sensual appetite. These help moisten the skin and are anti-aging, antioxidant, anti-inflammatory, and good for the gut. See *Love Buds Green Power Powder* on Ch.2, pg.23-24.

Kohlrabi
36 calories per cup and 5 grams of fiber. Kohlrabi is loaded with Vitamin C, minerals, and potassium; it fights cancer and is also great for weight loss. It's sweet, juicy, and crunchy; eat either raw or baked like an apple, with the sweetest edible greens. Green (mild) and purple (spicy) stems and leaves are great eaten raw and used for wraps.

Mushrooms (including Maitake, Oyster, Reishi, Shiitake & Cremini)
40 calories and 3 grams of fiber in 1 cup. The mushrooms listed here are among the top five for health benefits. Mushrooms are loaded with Vitamins B and D2, enzymes and 8 essential amino acids. They help strengthen the immune system, fight cancer and tumors, eliminate toxins, and are an antioxidant, antiviral and antibacterial. Mushrooms help reduce pain and nausea, fight anemia, stabilize blood sugar, and help lower cholesterol and blood pressure. See http://bit.ly/1dH92FT for more information. It is recommended to cook mushrooms for safe consumption.

Onions, Chives, Scallions and Shallots
60 calories in 1 cup. Rich in fiber. (The leading onions: Vidalia sweet onions, grown in Georgia and Walla Walla sweet onions, grown in Washington State.) Onions fight esophageal, stomach and prostate cancer. They help build strong bones, lower cholesterol and blood pressure, and fight heart disease. They are anti-inflammatory, antibiotic and antiviral and can help reduce allergies. Dried onions provide similar benefits.

Tomatoes
40 calories and 2 grams of fiber in 1 medium tomato. Cook with some fat to release more lycopene. Vine-ripened tomatoes have twice the vitamins and minerals and taste better than hot house tomatoes. Rich in potassium, tomatoes protect against prostate and many other cancers; they protect the heart and help reduce blood pressure.

Third Top Super Stars

Artichoke 60 calories and 7 grams of fiber in 1 artichoke. Artichokes are loaded with vitamins and minerals. They promote liver cleansing and detoxification, stimulate bile to prevent indigestion and fight stomach pain, nausea and vomiting. Artichokes help lower cholesterol and prevent cardiovascular disease.

Arugula 5 calories and 1 gram of fiber in 1 cup. Arugula contains as much calcium as spinach. Loaded in folic acid, Vitamins A and K, it promotes strong bones, stabilizes clotting and helps to prevent lung, esophageal and gastrointestinal cancers. Has a peppery, mustard flavor that is mild but slightly bitter. Sauté the large leaves and save the small, tender leaves for salads.

Asparagus 30 calories and 3 grams of fiber in 1 cup (also contains 3 grams of sugar). High in vitamins and minerals. Asparagus strengthens the female reproductive organs, reduces menstrual cramps and increases milk production. It is often used as a diuretic, calms the mind and spirit, improves the mood and sharpens memory. Asparagus can increase feelings of love and compassion and promotes fertility and increased sperm count.

Bok Choy 20 calories and 1.7 grams of fiber in 1 cup, cooked or raw. This Chinese chard or cabbage is loaded with vitamins and minerals and is tasty sautéed, but don't overcook it - especially the leaves.

Cauliflower 13 calories and 3 grams of fiber in 1 cup of flowerets. An antioxidant and detoxifier, cauliflower is anti-bacterial and anti-viral. It contains Vitamins C and the B-complex as well as manganese, copper, iron, calcium and potassium. Cauliflower fights prostate, breast, cervical, colon and ovarian cancer, and boosts the immune system. Use in place of potatoes.

Celery Root Like potatoes without the starch. Great for juicing. See celery

Eggplant 42 calories and 3 grams of fiber in 2 slices. Eggplant is an antioxidant, lowers cholesterol and high in vitamins and minerals.

Endive 10 calories and ½ gram of fiber in 10 leaves. Its sister vegetable, Escarole, is less bitter. This mega-vitamin and beta-carotene loaded vegetable makes for a great wrap or leafy cup for egg, tuna or chicken salad.

Fennel and fennel oil 27 calories in ½-cup. An antioxidant, loaded in calcium, magnesium, phosphorus and potassium. Soothes the gut, relieves gas, cramps, and aids digestion.

Green Beans 10 calories and 2 grams of fiber in ½ cup. Vitamins and minerals are released when slightly cooked. Contains folic acid; reduces the risk of heart disease, stroke, dementia and vascular disease.

Jerusalem Artichoke (sun choke) 72 calories and a trace of fiber in a ½ cup. A probiotic, Jerusalem artichokes fight constipation and colon cancer, promotes a healthy gut, and helps to lower cholesterol. If eaten raw it can cause gas in some people. Delicious when baked, resembles a gnarly potato or piece of ginger. Steam like a potato, peel, slice and enjoy.

Jicama 45 calories and 6 grams of fiber in 1 jicama. Loaded with Vitamins C and A and beta carotene. Fresh and crunchy, makes a great dipping vessel and snack.

Kava Root 30 calories and 1 gram of fiber in 1-2 tablespoons. Kava Root is considered the "feel good" vegetable. Reduces stress and anxiety, keeps the mind calm and clear with increased concentration. Kava root helps with asthma, urinary tract infections, depression, menopausal symptoms and muscle spasms.

Leeks 28 calories and 1 gram of fiber in ½ cup. Leeks are loaded with fiber and vitamins. They protect against prostrate and colon cancer, blood clots, strokes, macular degeneration and promotes cardiovascular health and eye strength.

Maca 20 calories and 1 gram of fiber in 1 tablespoon. Maca is a relative of the radish, and can be roasted or baked. Maca helps relieve chronic fatigue syndrome and enhances energy, stamina, and memory. It assists in fertility and female hormone balance, relieves menstrual problems and symptoms of menopause. Helps strengthen weak bones, alleviates depression, fights stomach cancer, leukemia, AIDS, and tuberculosis. It helps with erectile dysfunction, stimulates sexual desire, and boosts the immune system. See http://www.peoplelovebuds.com and http://www.lovebudspiceblends.com to purchase *Canna Maca Happy Powder*.

Okra 13 calories and 1.6 grams of fiber in ½ cup. An antioxidant, okra is high in Vitamins A, B, C and K, folic acid, and many minerals. It provides immune support and liver detoxification.

Parsley 4 calories in 1 tablespoon. Not just a garnish, parsley is loaded with Vitamins A and C, potassium and calcium. Protects against cancer, high blood pressure, and promotes strong bones and weight loss. Use it in salads and recipes for added flavor and health benefits.

Parsnips 100 calories and 5½ grams of fiber in 1 cooked cup. Parsnips are loaded with calcium, magnesium, folic acid and potassium, and protect against inflammation and cancer. Use parsnips in place of potatoes.

Peppers 4 calories in 2 tablespoons. Bell peppers are low in calories, but full of minerals and mega-vitamins, especially A, C and K. They help build bone strength and the immune system, and also lower the risk of prostate and lung cancers.

Peppers (hot) 7 calories and 1 gram of fiber in 1 tablespoon. Habaneros, jalapenos, chipotle, and poblanos, hot peppers are full of vitamins, minerals and fiber; provide pain relief, and help reduce inflammation. The smaller the pepper, the more potent it is and the more heat it contains. Red, yellow, orange and green peppers are loaded in vitamins and minerals but eating too many nightshade vegetables might irritate arthritis.

Pumpkin 42 calories and 3½ grams of fiber in 1 cooked cup. High in vitamins and minerals, especially beta carotene and potassium, pumpkins are highly antioxidant. Pumpkin lowers the risk of stroke, relieves muscle cramps, fights lung and colon cancer, and supports bone density, eye health and weight loss.

Rhubarb 94 calories and 4 grams of fiber in 1 cooked cup. Loaded in Vitamin C, calcium and magnesium.

Rutabagas 30 calories and a small amount of fiber in ½ cup. Rutabagas contain Vitamin C and potassium and fight various cancers. These veggies are good boiled, mashed, steamed, baked, cubed and pureed.

Snow Peas 80 calories and 5 grams of fiber per cup. Snow peas are high in Vitamins C, K and A, beta carotene, calcium, potassium and folic acid. The supports eye health. Eat raw or slightly stir-fried.

Squash 115 calories and 5-10 grams of fiber in 1 cooked cup. Including butternut, pumpkin and acorn squash, these are high in vitamins, minerals, and beta-carotene. Squash supports weight loss (use a low-sugar squash such as spaghetti squash), and is good for all digestive disorders.

Sweet Potatoes 120 calories and 4 grams of fiber in 1 cooked cup. Contains Vitamins B6, C and D, iron, potassium and magnesium. Sweet potatoes help lower blood pressure and aids in the prevention of heart attacks. Helps with bone and tooth and blood cell formation and digestion. They promote youthful skin and elasticity, and helps in coping with stress. They boost the energy level and mood. Limit these if weight loss is your goal. Remember that white potatoes act and digest like sugar (and sugar equals stored fat).

Turnips 35 calories and 3 grams of fiber in 1 cup. Turnips contain potassium, Vitamins C, A, and K, and calcium. Eat raw shredded turnips for a digestive aid and detoxification. They're also great cooked.

Vegetable Tips & Recommendations:

Add oranges to your greens to help absorb the nutrients. Be mindful of proper food pairing; make sure there is no protein, fat or grain present when combining fruits and vegetables.

Chapter 4: Choosing Foods to Better Support your Health Concerns

The food list at *Love Buds Spice Blends* is nutritious, healthy and balanced. Try to shop from the entire list unless you are sensitive, allergic, or have a strong dislike for a certain food. Enjoying your meals is the key to survival in a healthy life.

What ails you? Where do your concerns lie?

Below you will find over 60 health concerns and ailments that might be of interest to you. When you locate your area of interest you may find some foods not to your liking; foods which may provoke sensitivities or allergies, or foods not in your diet or within your doctor's recommendation. The foods listed are from many years of study and research in the specific area. There are so many studies, theories and ideas that it is very difficult to know what to choose. At the end of the book is a list of the sources used for this information.

As a first step forward, we suggest you read, ask people you trust, try various food choices for a while, and take the best of five choices. Always ask your physician before trying any new program, and keep in mind these are only recommendations. As noted in the introduction, this cookbook is not meant to be taken as medical advice, and the author is not a medically-trained professional.

Why are these health conditions grouped together the way they are?

We've grouped these health conditions according to whether or not they share similar food recommendations. They may not be otherwise related.

Anti-Aging, Alzheimer's, Brain & Memory Function

> Initial Tips: Each day, include dark greens and yellow fruits, particularly apricots. Also eat carrots, pumpkin, spinach, squash (winter), sweet potatoes, grapefruit, oranges, tangerines, mackerel, salmon and tuna.

Follow the recommendations under
Diabetic Diet
Including:

Beverages & Smoothies Acai, barley grass, cranberry juice or concentrate, cocoa, coffee, red wine, fruit and vegetable juices. When juicing, add 2 tablespoons of fish or flaxseed oil. Add *Canna Super Green Power Powder* or *Canna Maca Happy Powder* (Ch.2, pg.23-24) to juice and smoothies. Enjoy black, green and white teas. See the tea list (Ch.2, pg.25-27) for more tasty blends.

Dairy Goat cheese and yogurt

Fats Almond & peanut butter, ghee, coconut, olive, macadamia & Omega-3 oils

Nuts PAW (pecans, almonds, walnuts), hazelnuts, filberts, flax seeds, macadamia, small amount of peanuts, pumpkin, roasted sesame and sunflower seeds

Fruit Apples, cantaloupe, watermelon, berries, blackberries, blueberries, cherries, cranberries, dates, grapes, guava, kiwi, lemon, oranges, papaya, prune, raspberries, star fruit and strawberries

Grains Wheat germ, cracked or sprouted wheat, spelt, oatmeal and quinoa

Legumes Black beans, edamame, garbanzo beans, kidney beans, lentils, peas, pinto and red beans

Protein Whey is a superior protein as are salmon, mackerel and sardines
Second choice: cod, clams, chicken, lamb, liver, oysters, scallops and turkey
Third choice: wild game

Rice Brown and wild rice occasionally; stay true to pairing.

Vegetables Arugula, asparagus roots, avocado, beets, broccoli, Brussel sprouts, cabbage, carrots, cauliflower, dandelion greens and roots, green beans, kale, kava root, kimchi, leafy greens, leeks, maca, mushrooms, okra, onions, peppers, pumpkin, fresh sauerkraut, scallions, shallots, spinach, squash, sweet potatoes, tomatoes.

Spices and Condiments Chives, cocoa, garlic, ginger, orange peel blossom, oregano, parsley, rosemary, sage, thyme and turmeric; also see the *Canna Spice Blends* (Ch.2, pg.21-23).

Anxiety, Bi-Polar Disorder, Depression & Insomnia

Initial Tips: For treating insomnia, warm milk and kava root keep the mind calm and clear. Hypertension may be better regulated by including olive oil mixed with lettuce, celery and carrots.

Follow the recommendations under
Anti-Aging and Gastrointestinal Health
Including:

Beverages Acai and cranberry juice daily. Add *Canna Super Green Power Powder* or *Canna Maca Happy Powder* (Ch.2, pg.23-24) to juice and smoothies. Enjoy black, green and white teas. See the tea list (Ch.2, pg.25-27) for more tasty blends.

Dairy Yogurt

Fats and Nuts ghee, sesame seeds, PAW (pecans, almonds, walnut)

Fruit eat blueberries first thing in the morning to boost your mood hormone; this can help cheer you up when you're feeling sad. Cranberries and strawberries dipped in dark chocolate boost serotonin and endorphin levels. Bananas and all melons are also good.

Spices garlic, oregano, saffron, wheat germ, *Canna Italian and French Spice Blends*.

Sweeteners raisins, dates, stevia and xylitol

Vegetables asparagus root, celery, dandelion root and greens, maca, mushrooms reishi, pumpkin and tomatoes (cooked).

Autoimmune Illnesses, Cancer, & Nausea

Initial Tips: Enjoy soft, mild sandwiches to soothe the stomach & intestines. Soups, casseroles & steamed, soft foods help as well. Include resveratrol for body repair & anti-cancer activity (found in dark grapes, red wine, cherries, plums & peanuts). Avoid processed meat, potato chips, beans, nuts & legumes

Beverages Acai berry, broth, cranberry, red wine, plain bouillon and pomegranate are the best choices. Add *Canna Super Green Power Powder* or *Canna Maca Happy Powder* (Ch.2, pg.23-24) to juice and smoothies. Enjoy black, green and white teas. See the tea list (Ch.2, pg.25-27) for more tasty blends.

Dairy Cheese, French goat cheese, milk and yogurt

Fats Butter, flaxseed oil, ghee, low-fat mayonnaise, extra virgin olive oil, Omega-3 fatty acids, nuts in small amounts, almonds, ground flax seeds, macadamia nuts and oil, peanuts, walnuts and smooth peanut butter

Fruit Apple, apricot, avocado, bananas, blueberries, cherries, citrus fruit, coconut in small amounts, cranberries, grapefruit, grapes, guava, kiwi, lemon, orange, papaya, peaches, pineapple, prunes, raspberries, strawberries and tangerines

Grains Oatmeal and quinoa

Hard Candy 10-40 calories per piece. Hard candy soothes the mouth and throat, alleviates dry mouth, and aids digestion.

Legume Beans and lentils Beans are so good for you, but if they give you gas this might not be a good time to eat them. Soy, miso, tempeh, tofu and mung beans are more soothing to the gut.

Marmalade 60 calories in 1 tablespoon. Soothes mouth and throat; helps with digestion and dry mouth

Protein Use only tender cuts of meat, baked or broiled, poached but not fried, or items such as meatloaf or a tender roast. Use chicken & turkey (light or ark) or wild game. Eggs are a great source of protein and always a top choice. Stew, boil, bake or poach fish and seafood including sardines, shellfish, salmon and tuna.

Rice Brown rice

Spices, Herbs and Condiments Mild or sweet chili peppers, cinnamon, cloves (cooked), cocoa, cumin, garlic, ginger, horseradish in small amounts, ketchup, olives, mustard seed, mild mustard, onions, oregano, parsley, rosemary, mild salad dressing, turmeric. Also see the *Canna Spice Blends* (Ch.2, pg.21-23).

Sweeteners Bee propolis, chocolate, clear jelly, hard candy, honey, licorice, marmalade, syrup, stevia and xylitol

Vegetables Arugula, beets, broccoli, broccoli rabe, Brussel sprouts, cabbage, carrots, cauliflower, celery, collard greens, fennel, Jerusalem artichoke, kale, kimchi, leeks, mushrooms, onions, peas, peppers, pumpkin, rutabagas, sauerkraut, turnips, sea vegetables (dried), spinach, squash (especially pumpkin and acorn), sweet potatoes without the skins, tomatoes (cooked), turnips and watercress.

Diabetes & Sugars

It isn't just the sugar, it's what turns into sugar

Initial Tips:

- Enjoy a high fiber breakfast. Eat 5-8 small meals a day; add veggies, 1 cup of beans a day, and fiber 4 to 5 times daily. The beans will help to both lower cholesterol and blood sugar. Check your weight (and stay on top of it). Have salad before every meal, with apple cider vinegar. Snacks can be things like sugar-free popsicles, pie and cookies. There are sugar-free bakery products for diabetics which help a lot if you have a sweet tooth. Have absolutely no refined sugar or white flour, and stay away from most grains.

- Unless your blood sugar is stable, we recommend eliminating any starch: grains, rice, starchy vegetables like sweet potatoes, squash, beets and bananas. It's very important to follow the food pairing guide when eating grains like pasta or sandwiches

- Remember, always enjoy fruit, fruit juices & wine on an empty stomach and do not eat again for at least one hour

Beverage Acai berry & coffee. Three or more cups per day will help process the sugar and reduce the risk of diabetes. Fruit juices (especially Cranberry) and vegetable juices are great choices. Add 2 tablespoons Omega-3 oils to your beverages. Add *Canna Super Green Power Powder* or *Canna Maca Happy Powder* (Ch.2, pg.23-24) to juice and smoothies. Enjoy black, green and white teas. See the tea list (Ch.2, pg.25-27) for more tasty blends. Enjoy red wines and other foods containing resveratrol.

Dairy Cream cheese, feta goat cheese, ricotta cheese and yogurt

Fats and Nuts Raw almonds and peanut butter, flax seeds, PAW (pecan, almonds, walnuts), and seeds.

> First Choice: Blackberries, cherries, grapefruit, lemon, lime, raspberries and tomato

> Second Choice: Apples, apricots, avocado, blueberry, avocado, figs, guava, mango, nectarines, oranges, peaches, pears, pineapple, plumbs, prunes, raspberries, strawberries, tomatoes and watermelon.

> Third Choice: Dried apricots, bananas, cantaloupe, kiwi & melons.

Grains Pure fiber bread, brewer's yeast, bran flakes, buckwheat, rolled steel cut oats, pasta, quinoa. Substitute ½ of the flour in recipes with wheat germ.

Legumes

> First Choice: Black beans, edamame, garbanzo, lentils, peas and soy beans
> Second Choice: Lima, kidney, chickpea and white beans, black-eyed peas

Protein Cod, eggs, game meat, mackerel, salmon, sardine (canned), Bluefin tuna and turkey. Each serving should be equal to the size of your palm.

Rice Brown and wild rice, no white or white blend rice

Spice and condiments We have found that various spices and herbs are important for diabetic control. Use chives, cinnamon, dark chocolate, cocoa, garlic, olives, parsley, sage, and turmeric. Look for these same ingredients in many of our *Canna Spice Blends* in Ch.2, pg.21-23.

Sweeteners Dates and honey are good sweeteners, but if you react to them, use stevia or xylitol. Other sweeteners and sweet food additions include licorice, peanut butter, raisins, cinnamon, nutmeg and vanilla.

Vegetables

> First Choice: Alfalfa sprouts, artichoke, arugula, asparagus, broccoli, Brussel sprouts, cabbage, cauliflower, celery, chili peppers, chives, cucumber, dandelion root extract and leaf, fennel, Jerusalem artichoke, leafy greens, leeks, lettuce, maca, mushrooms, mustard, greens, okra, onions, parsley, bell & hot peppers, sea vegetables, spinach, acorn & butternut squash limit to low sugar squash, watercress and zucchini.
>
> Second Choice: Carrots, eggplant and raw green beans. The glycemic load of a carrot is only 3 so diabetics can eat them safely. Combine with a little fat, spinach and broccoli to lessen the sugar.
>
> Third Choice: Peas, red beets and sweet potatoes.

Eye Health

The best way to cope with the health of your eyes is to maintain a nutritious diet filled with lots of protein & vegetables

Follow the recommendations under
Antioxidant and Diabetic Diet
Including:

Beverages Red Clover Blossom Tea. Add *Canna Super Green Power Powder* or *Canna Maca Happy Powder* (Ch.2, pg.23-24) to juice and smoothies. Enjoy black, green and white teas. See the tea list (Ch.2, pg.25-27) for more tasty blends.

Fruit Blueberries, kiwi, papaya and peaches.

Protein Eggs, salmon and whey protein.

Spices Cocoa, parsley and turmeric.

Vegetables Avocado, broccoli, carrots, collard greens, dandelion root, leaf and extracts, green beans, kale, leeks, pumpkin, snow peas, spinach, summer squash, Swiss chard, tomatoes cooked in rich fat, turnips, raw greens and watercress.

Constipation, Diverticular Disease, Gallbladder Gastrointestinal Health, Obesity & Weight loss

Tips & Recommendations:

A healthy gut is the lifeline to greater health.

- Begin each day with lemonade made of 12 ounces of water, I lemon quartered, and 1 teaspoon stevia. Puree; strain if you wish, and enjoy!
- Detox with fiber and water, and then more water.
- Ginger, lemon and fennel soothe stomach and gut irritations.
- Have 6-8 small meals each day.
- When eating eggs include the yolks; they help to break down fat.
- Whey is the best protein source for optimum digestion, absorption of nutrients and to gain muscle and lose fat.
- Poultry should be prepared without the skin for fewer calories and increased digestion power.
- Mushrooms are a lifesaver for health benefits and are a tasty, filling, low-calorie food.
- One cup of beans per day can lower cholesterol and inflammation by 10% or more, as well as help relieve heart burn, indigestion, constipation, diarrhea and inflammation.
- It is true that an apple a day keeps the doctor away!
- Include probiotic fuel 2-3 times each week or more.
- If you are on a weight loss plan, try to keep your snacks below 100 calories. carrot, celery, radishes, jicama, and peanut butter with a veggie dip and fruit, low-fat cheese, and low- or no-sugar bars are good choices.
- No overeating as this can create gas, a sluggish system or even blockage. Give your digestive system a daily fast of 12 overnight hours (for example, from 7 p.m. to 7 a.m). If you are an early riser and need to eat right away, then stop your food intake earlier in the evening.

Beverages Aloe vera juice, barley grass juice, fruit and vegetable juices with 2 tablespoons Omega3, 2 capsules of fiber and 2 tablespoons of psyllium. Add *Canna Super Green Power Powder* or *Canna Maca Happy Powder* (Ch.2, pg.23-24) to juice and smoothies. Enjoy black, green and white teas. See the tea list (Ch.2, pg.25-27) for more tasty blends.

Dairy Yogurt delivers live active cultures to the gut. The probiotic found in Greek yogurt does a better job when paired with bananas and whole grains (an exception to the rule of food pairing).

Fats Butter, coconut, ghee, flax, fish, Omega-3 oils and nuts.

Nuts PAW (pecans, almonds and walnut), flax and ground sesame seeds.

Fruits Apple, apricots (not dried), banana, blackberries, blueberries, cantaloupe, cherries, figs, grapefruit, gogi berries, guava, honeydew melon, kiwi, orange, papayas, pineapple, prunes, raspberries, star fruit and watermelon.

Grain Barley, bran, spelt, wheat bran, quinoa, wheat germ (follow the food pairing requirements).

Legumes Black beans, chickpeas, garbanzo, green peas, kidney beans, lentils, miso, mung, navy, peas, pinto, red beans and tempeh.

Protein Chicken, cod, eggs, flounder, grouper, haddock, wild halibut, herring, lamb, mackerel, Mahi-Mahi, orange roughy, salmon, sardines, shrimp, swordfish, clams, oysters and muscles, tilapia, turkey, Bluefin tuna, whey protein and wild game.

Rice Brown and wild rice (follow the food pairing outline).

Sesame seeds These seeds contain zinc and Vitamin E. They are good for the heart and help promote eye, hair and skin health. Sesame seeds also help burn fat, support healthy bones, help lower blood pressure, reduce cholesterol and help combat diabetes. Eat sunflower seeds directly from the shell for weight loss.

Spices Allspice, black pepper, cardamom, chili powder, chlorella powder, cilantro, cinnamon, cocoa, cumin, ginger, horseradish, mustard seed, olives, oregano, saffron and thyme. Also see the *Canna Spice Blends* (Ch.2, pg.21-23).

Sweeteners Licorice, raisins, dates, honey, xylitol and stevia.

Vegetables Artichoke, arugula, asparagus and asparagus root, beets, broccoli, Brussel sprouts, cabbage red and purple, carrots, cauliflower, celery & celery root, dandelion greens, root & root extract, fennel, Jerusalem artichoke, jicama, kimchi, maca, mushrooms, parsley, hot and mild peppers, pumpkins, fresh sauerkraut, spinach, acorn and butternut squash, cooked tomatoes, raw turnips, turnip greens and watercress.

Headaches & Migraines

The best way to cope with headaches is to maintain a nutritious diet filled with lots of protein & vegetables.

Follow the Food List for
Antioxidant and Diabetic food groups
Including:

Beverages Very cold and very hot beverages. Add *Canna Super Green Power Powder* or *Canna Maca Happy Powder* (Ch.2, pg.23-24) to juice and smoothies. Enjoy black, green and white teas. See the tea list (Ch.2, pg.25-27) for more tasty blends.

Dairy Cottage cheese and yogurt.

Fruit Apples, apricots, blueberries, cherries, lemons, limes and oranges.

Legumes and Beans All beans including snap beans.

Protein Low fat meat and poultry; no pork.

Vegetables Artichokes, broccoli, carrots, celery, mushrooms, peas and sweet potatoes.

Blood Pressure, Cardiovascular, Cholesterol & Healthy Heart

Follow the Food List for
Gastrointestinal and Diabetic Health
Including:

Beverages Add *Canna Super Green Power Powder* or *Canna Maca Happy Powder* (Ch.2, pg.23-24) to juice and smoothies. Enjoy black, green and white teas. See the tea list (Ch.2, pg.25-27) for more tasty blends.

Fruit Apples, apricots, avocado, bananas, figs, grapefruit, oranges papayas, prunes

Dairy Low-fat milk

Grains Bran and oats

Legumes and Beans Include daily

Protein Fish, especially mackerel and salmon, shellfish, spinach, tofu and tuna

Vegetables Brussel sprouts, cauliflower, edamame, mushrooms, onions and potatoes

Fats Chestnuts

Crohn's Disease, Irritable Bowel Disease (IBD) Irritable Bowel Syndrome (IBS)

Initial Tips: Cramps, diarrhea and inflammation are a delicate balancing act of many uncomfortable issues and symptoms. Only you can decide what is best for your symptoms. Keep a daily journal, including a list of different fluids and amounts, foods (including spices), fats (including the Omega fatty acid), exercise and rest time. Keep this information precise and up to date so that you can reference it as your symptoms change.

Follow the Food Lists for
Gastrointestinal and Diabetic Health & Immune Support
Including:

Beverage Add *Canna Super Green Power Powder* or *Canna Maca Happy Powder* (Ch.2, pg.23-24) to juice and smoothies. Enjoy black, green and white teas. See the tea list (Ch.2, pg.25-27) for more tasty blends.

Dairy Possibly nonfat milk and yogurt.

Fats Ghee, clarified butter

Grains White rice, when eaten with yogurt, helps to combat diarrhea.

Fruit For constipation, add fiber and watery fruits including apples, pears, pineapple. For diarrhea, add bananas.

Legumes and Beans Eat in small amounts until you know you can tolerate them. Try soy, miso, tempeh, tofu, beans for a smoother digestion

Protein Salmon and other easy-to-digest proteins like eggs.

Spices Black pepper, cardamom seeds, chlorella powder, cinnamon, ginger, maca, mustard seed, periwinkle herb. Add our *Canna* Green Powders (Ch.2, pg.23-24) to your juices and smoothies as needed.

Vegetables Carrots, hot peppers, pumpkin, fennel, acorn and butternut squash, spinach, sweet potatoes and ginger.

Aids, Anemia, HIV Hepatitis, Herpes & Immune System

Follow the Food Lists for
Antioxidant, Diabetes, Detox, All Super Foods
Including:

Beverages Acai berry juice, coffee, cranberry & pomegranate juice, fruit & vegetable juices. Add *Canna Super Green Power Powder* or *Canna Maca Happy Powder* (Ch.2, pg.23-24) to juice and smoothies. Enjoy black, green and white teas. See the tea list (Ch.2, pg.25-27) for more tasty blends.

Dairy Yogurt

Fats Coconut, macadamia, olive and walnut oils, almonds, Brazil nuts, macadamia nuts, pistachio nuts, walnuts, pumpkin and roasted sunflower seeds.

Fruits apricots, blueberries, cantaloupe, coconut, goji, honeydew, kiwi, papaya, pineapple, raspberries, strawberries, tangerines and watermelon.

Grains Bulgur, bran, oats, quinoa and wheat germ.

Legumes Black beans, chick peas, garbanzo, snap beans and lentils.

Protein Clams, cod, eggs, fish, mussels, oysters, salmon, scallops, tuna, wild game and whey protein.

Spices Cinnamon, clove, cocoa, cumin, garlic, ginger, horseradish, olives, oregano, parsley, pepper, peppermint, rosemary and turmeric. Also see our *Canna Spice Blends* for more information Ch.2, pg.21-23.

Sweeteners Bee propolis, honey, licorice, black strap molasses, stevia and xylitol.

Vegetables Artichoke, beets, cabbage, carrots, cauliflower, dandelion greens, endive, escarole, jicama, kimchi, maca, mushrooms (maitake, shiitake, rishi), okra, onions, and peppers, parsley, rhubarb, fresh sauerkraut, sea vegetables, spinach, sprouts, acorn and butternut squash, Swiss chard and watercress.

Women's Health
Cholesterol, Healthy Heart, Hormones Menopause, PMS, Reproduction & Urology

Use any foods from the master food list

Initial Tips:
- Try to eat 2 servings of seafood such as wild salmon, pollock, cod, canned light tuna, catfish or shrimp each day.
- Use Passion Flower Tea for pain, insomnia, cramps, childbirth pain and inflammation.
- Hypertension may be better regulated by including olive oil mixed with lettuce, celery, carrots and resveratrol daily.
- Ginger tea eases morning sickness and PMS; ginger lemon tea is good for cold hands and feet.

Beverages Coffee for overall health; it also aids with cramps and mood. Drink fruit and vegetable juices, adding 3 tablespoons of Omega-3; ginger and lemon, pomegranate and cranberry juice. Add *Canna Super Green Power Powder* or *Canna Maca Happy Powder* (Ch.2, pg.23-24) to juice and smoothies. Enjoy black, green and white teas. See the tea list (Ch.2, pg.25-27) for more tasty blends.

Dairy Cottage cheese, goat cheese, yogurt and skim milk for PMS

Fats Butter, coconut oil (helps reduce pelvic issues), flax seed and macadamia oil, low fat mayonnaise and peanut butter, PAW (pecans, almonds and walnuts), peanuts, pumpkin, sesame and roasted sunflower seeds.

Fruit Eat blueberries first thing in the morning to boost your mood; bananas, blueberries, cantaloupe, cherries, cranberries, figs, dark red or purple grapes, guava, honeydew melon, kiwi, lemon, pineapple, raspberries, strawberries and watermelon.

Grains Whole, cracked, or sprouted wheat, quinoa, spelt and oatmeal.

Legumes and Beans Chick peas, garbanzo beans, humus, green peas, kidney, lentils, navy, pinto and red beans.

Soy Tempeh (tastes, cooks and acts like mushrooms).

Protein Extra-lean beef, catfish, cod, eggs, fish (including canned or fresh salmon), pollack, poultry, sardines, shellfish, shrimp, tuna and turkey.

Rice Brown and wild

Spices and Condiments Chives, cinnamon, cocoa, garlic, ginger, ginkgo biloba, gravel root, oregano, parsley, rosemary, sage, tomato sauce and turmeric. See our Canna Spice Blends in Ch.2, pgs.21-23 for more.

Sweeteners Dates, chocolate, cocoa, honey, licorice, raisins, stevia and xylitol.

Vegetables Artichoke, arugula, asparagus, avocado, beets, broccoli, broccoli rabe, red and purple cabbage, carrots, celery, chives, dandelion root extract and greens, green beans, Jerusalem artichoke, kale, kimchi, leeks, maca, mushrooms (malaki, shiitake and reishi), okra, onions, parsley, bell & hot peppers, pumpkin, fresh sauerkraut, scallions, shallots, spinach, sweet potatoes and cooked tomatoes.

Men's Health
Blood Pressure, Cholesterol, Healthy Heart
Prostrate, Testosterone & Urology

Initial Tips:
- Have a daily dose of resveratrol (found in red wine, grapes, cherries, peanuts, blueberries, pumpkin seeds and cranberries).
- Increase fluids, but reduce caffeine and beer.
- Use sea salt only.
- Weight management is critical: limit red meat for weight and heart health.
- Eat 1 cup of beans to help reduce cholesterol.
- Selenium is a beneficial mineral found in nuts - especially Brazil nuts; seafood, fish, wheat bran, wheat germ, oats and brown rice. Selenium is an antioxidant, and may help prevent prostate cancer, heart disease and rheumatoid arthritis; promotes a balanced thyroid.
- Hypertension might be better regulated by including olive oil mixed with lettuce, celery and carrots.
- Avoid hard alcohol and spicy foods.

Follow the Food List for
Antioxidant, Diabetes and Gastrointestinal Health Food Groups
including:

Beverages Acai, fruit and vegetable juices, cranberry & pomegranate juice. Add *Canna Super Green Power Powder* or *Canna Maca Happy Powder* (Ch.2, pg.23-24) to juice and smoothies. Enjoy black, green and white teas. See the tea list (Ch.2, pg.25-27) for more tasty blends.

Dairy Low fat, goat cheese and yogurt.

Fats Almond butter, coconut, flax seed, macadamia oil, olive oil, Omega-3 oils and peanut butter.

Nuts PAW (pecan, almonds and walnuts), flax seed, hazelnuts, filberts, macadamia and peanut butter, peanuts, pistachio, pumpkin, sesame seeds and sunflower seeds.

Fruit Eat blueberries first thing in the morning to boost your mood hormone. Cantaloupe, coconut, cranberry, pink and red grapefruit, dark red or purple grapes, guava, honeydew melon, pineapple, strawberries and watermelon. Choose bright-colored fruits as much as possible.

Grains Cracked, sprouted and spelt wheat, oatmeal, quinoa and wheat germ.

Legumes and Beans Chick peas, garbanzo beans, green peas, kidney, lentils, navy, north, pinto and red beans.

Soy Edamame, miso and tempeh.

Protein Eggs (include the yolks), fish high in Omega-3 oils, oysters, and skinless poultry, salmon, sardines, turkey and wild game.

Rice Brown and wild.

Spices Chives, cinnamon, cocoa, garlic, ginger, olives, oregano, rosemary and sage. See our Canna Spice Blends in Ch.2, pg.21-23 for more.

Sweeteners Dates, dark chocolate, licorice, raisins, stevia and xylitol.

Vegetables Artichoke, asparagus, avocado, beets, broccoli, Brussel sprouts, red and purple cabbage, carrots, cauliflower, celery, dandelion root and greens, green beans, Jerusalem artichoke, kale, kimchi, leeks, mushrooms (maitake, shiitake and reishi), onions, bell and hot peppers, pumpkin, fresh sauerkraut, scallions, shallots, spinach, cooked tomatoes (tomatoes cooked with a little fat release more lycopene for greater benefits; eat them 2-3 times a week.).

Fibromyalgia, Multiple Sclerosis, Nerve Disorders, Parkinson's Disease & Seizures

Follow the Food Lists for
Gastrointestinal, Diabetes and Immune System

These three food lists will cover everything you need for these illnesses.

Tips & Recommendations:

Add *Canna Super Green Power Powder* or *Canna Maca Happy Powder* (Ch.2, pg.23-24) to juice and smoothies. Enjoy black, green and white teas. See the tea list (Ch.2, pg.25-27) for more tasty blends.

- Best food recommendations: dark colored fruits and vegetables, raspberries, blackberries, spinach, leafy green veggies, broccoli, tomatoes, carrots, garlic, red kidney beans, pinto beans, cranberries, strawberries, plums and apples. Lots of green and black teas, red wine and dark juices. Omega-3 fatty acids as found in mackerel, sardines, tuna, salmon, yogurt and milk.

- Maintain a nutritious diet filled with lots of protein and vegetables, including daily servings of eggs, blueberries, coffee and tea.

Inflammation, Osteoarthritis & Pain

Initial Tips:
- When using cannabis, the CBD compound is good for discomfort and inflammation; the THC compound is good for pain.
- Limit alcohol; avoid grilled, fried and processed meat, fried and processed foods, and animal fat.
- Make sure your diet contains resveratrol, Omega-3 fatty acids, the "Super Foods" listed above, and Vitamin D.
- Manage your weight. Keep your weight at or below the recommended level to avoid straining your bones and joints.
- The recommend diet for any pain, inflammation or joint stress is to follow the Mediterranean Diet or eat Asian foods. You can ease your pain and inflammation by going vegan or vegetarian.
- Add *Canna Super Green Power Powder* and *Canna Maca Powder* to your juice and smoothies to help fight inflammation.
- For chronic conditions, avoid nightshade vegetables such as tomatoes, eggplant, potatoes, gogi berries and peppers.

Follow the Food Lists for
Rheumatoid Arthritis, Auto Immune Illness, Gastrointestinal Illnesses & Diabetes
Including:

Beverages Acai berry juice, aloe Vera juice, coffee, fruit and vegetable juices (add 3 tablespoons of Omega-3 oil), tea (especially ginger green and passion flower). Add *Canna Super Green Power Powder* or *Canna Maca Happy Powder* (Ch.2, pg.23-24) to juice and smoothies. Enjoy black, green and white teas. See the tea list (Ch.2, pg.25-27) for more tasty blends.

Dairy Cream, ghee, cheese, whole milk and yogurt. Many people who suffer with arthritis do very well with dairy products; others sometimes do poorly. Only you will know what's right for you. Try to keep a journal and see for yourself.

Fats Butter, coconut oil, cod liver oil, ghee, fish and flax seed oil, macadamia and olive oil, Omega-3 fatty acids, sesame and walnut oils.

Nuts PAW (pecan, almond and walnuts), peanuts and sesame seeds.

Fruits All fruits, especially apples, cherries, papaya, pineapple, raisins and raspberries.

Grains Oatmeal, brewer's yeast, quinoa. Use wheat germ to replace half the flour in recipes.

Legumes and Beans Chick peas and garbanzo beans, miso and tempeh.

Protein Cod, eggs (including yolks), herring, lamb, liver, oily fish, mackerel, skinless poultry, salmon, shrimp, tuna, whey protein, and occasional wild game.

Spice Chili powder, chives, cinnamon, clove, cocoa, garlic, ginger, lemon juice, olives, oregano, parsley, rosemary, sage, thyme, turmeric and wasabi. See our *Canna Spice Blends* in Ch.2, pg. 21-23 for more.

Sweeteners Dates, gin-soaked golden raisins, chocolate (chocolate might cause inflammation in some women), licorice, raisins, molasses, stevia and xylitol.

Vegetables Alfalfa, asparagus root, red and purple cabbage, carrots, cauliflower, chives, dried fennel, garlic, kimchi, onions, parsley, bell and hot peppers, pumpkin, scallions, shallots, snow peas, spinach, acorn and butternut squash, red or yellow tomatoes. For chronic conditions, avoid nightshade vegetables such as tomatoes, eggplant, potatoes, gogi berries and peppers.

Rheumatoid Arthritis

The best way to cope with arthritis is to maintain a nutritious diet filled with lots of protein and vegetables.

Initial Tips:
- Follow an Asian diet, and include aloe vera juice, and whey protein. Some people may not be able to eat meat or legumes.
- Brew some cardamom tea daily by taking 2 teaspoons cardamom seeds, and bringing them to a boil for 5 minutes. Drain and discard the seeds and enjoy the drink.

Follow the Food List for
Pain, Inflammation and Immune Support
Including:

Beverages Add *Canna Super Green Power Powder* or *Canna Maca Happy Powder* (Ch.2, pg.23-24) to juice and smoothies. Enjoy black, green and white teas. See the tea list (Ch.2, pg.25-27) for more tasty blends.

Fruit Grapefruit, oranges and tangerines

Protein Mackerel, salmon, tuna and cantaloupe

Vegetables Broccoli and Brussel sprouts

Sensual Stimulant and Mood Boosting

Follow the food Lists for
Diabetes and Anti-Aging
Including:

Daily Smoothie Add Love Buds *Canna Super Green Power Powder* or *Canna Maca Happy Powder* (Ch.2, pg.23-24) into your daily smoothie blend.

Beverage Barley grass juice, apple cider, cranberry juice, red wine and tea including cardamom, clove, black, green and white teas. See the tea list (Ch.2, pg.25-27) for more tasty blends.

Fats Coconut oil.

Nuts PAW (pecans, almonds, walnuts), Brazil nuts, pine nuts, pumpkin and sesame seeds.

Grains Oatmeal, wheat bran and wheat germ.

Fruit Apples, blackberries, coconut, goji berries, peaches, red grapefruit and watermelon.

Legumes and Beans Edamame, miso and tempeh. (Soy can help prevent prostate enlargement.)

Protein Eggs, oysters, salmon, sardines, most seafood. Cut back or eliminate red meat.

Spices Cardamom, clove, chives, cocoa, garlic, mustard seed, olives, oregano, saffron and sea salt. Also see the *Canna Spice Blends* (Ch.2, pg.21-23).

Sweeteners Dates, honey, raisins, stevia and xylitol

Vegetables Arugula, asparagus, asparagus root, avocado, broccoli, celery, iceberg lettuce, maca, onions, hot peppers, spinach, tomatoes cooked with rich fat. Limit canned vegetables and eat fresh food whenever possible.

Anorexia, Energy, Stamina & Weight Gain

Initial Tips:
- Low potassium can cause muscle cramps. To burn belly and body fat, the formula is 20% exercise and 80% your food choices.

Follow the Food List
Anti-aging, Diabetes and Immune System
Including:

Beverages Coconut milk, goat milk and whole milk. Add *Canna Super Green Power Powder* or *Canna Maca Happy Powder* (Ch.2, pg.23-24) to juice and smoothies. Enjoy black, green and white teas. See the tea (Ch.2, pg.25-27) list for more tasty blends.

Dairy Cheese, whole milk and yogurt.

Fats Butter, ghee, extra virgin olive oil, peanut butter.

Nuts All nuts especially PAW (pecans, almonds and walnuts).

Fruits Bananas, coconut, dates and dried fruits.

Grains Cracked, spelt, or sprouted wheat; Ezekiel frozen wheat bread, quinoa, rolled and steel cut oats.

Legumes All legumes, especially green peas.

Protein Eggs, fish, lean meats, poultry (dark meat), salmon, shellfish, tuna and whey protein to gain muscle.

Rice Brown and wild.

Spices All spices; also see the *Canna Spice Blends* (Ch.2, pg.21-23).

Vegetables Avocados, carrots, broccoli, sweet potatoes, maca, mushrooms (reishi), pumpkin and squash.

NOTES

The Recipes

103. THE KITCHEN PANTRY
136. HYDRATION & LIBATIONS
160. BRUNCH WITH A PUNCH
201. NUTS ABOUT NUTS

213. THE DINNER TABLE
230. VEGETABLES
257. DESSERTS
287. REFERENCE LIST

I hope you enjoy the new journey of Cooking with Cannabis. When trying new recipes, it is best to follow the recipe as closely as possible and then make changes to suite your personal taste. For easy access, we have included note cards so you can remind yourself "to do next time" or "use this recipe."

Good Luck & Enjoy!

Cheryl

Chapter 5: The Kitchen Pantry

Dressings, Sauces and Marinades

104. Vegetable Base
(Vegan-Grain Friendly)
- 104. Bar-B-Que Sauce
- 104. Chick Pea Croutons
- 105. Cocktail Sauce
- 105. Garlic Thai Sauce
- 106. Ginger Sesame Dressing
- 106. Horseradish Chili Sauce
- 107. Hummus
- 107. Roasted Tomato Hummus
- 107. Jamaican Mustard
- 108. Jerk Sauce
- 108. Kiwi Compote
- 109. Lemon Pepper Dressing & Marinade
- 109. Lemon Dressing
- 109. Lemongrass Salad Dressing
- 110. Mustard Dill Salad Dressing
- 110. Mango Marinade, Salsa & Tenderizer
- 111. Soy Mushroom Sauce
- 111. Grilled Red Onions
- 111. Crispy Sage Onions
- 112. Fried Savory Onions
- 114. Quick & Easy Pizza Sauce
- 114. Pizza Sauce
- 114. Gin or Rum Raisin Nut Sauce
- 115. Black Bean Jerk Salsa
- 115. Cucumber Salsa
- 116. Chunky Taco Salsa
- 116. Hot Pepper Salsa
- 117. Spaghetti Sauce
- 117. Tahini Dressing
- 118. Tomato Vinaigrette & Marinade
- 118. Italian Red Wine Dressing
- 118. White Wine Dressing

Creamy Cooking Basics
- 120. Cream Skillet Sauté
- 120. Basic Roux
- 120. Coconut Cream
- 121. Spiced Cream
- 121. Milk
- 121. Coffee and Tea Creamer

Creamy Dressings & Toppings
- 122. Blue Cheese Dressing
- 123. Butter Garlic Cream Sauce
- 123. Creamy Cesar Dressing
- 124. Bake & Fry Blend
- 125. Jamaican Butter Cream Sauce
- 125. Cheese Mushroom Sauce
- 125. Pepper Cole Slaw Dressing
- 126. Bitter Sweet Cream Sauce
- 126. Cheese Sauce
- 126. Curry Dressing & Marinade
- 127. Dill Sauce
- 127. Goat Cheese Sprinkles
- 127. Greek Dressing & Marinade
- 128. Creamy Lemon Pepper Dressing
- 128. Fresh Lime Dressing
- 128. Curry or Lemon Mayonnaise
- 128. Savory Mayonnaise
- 129. Spicy Mayonnaise Butter Spread
- 129. Oven Fried Onions

Yogurt Dressings
- 129. Chili Salad Dressing & Marinade
- 131. Chinese Salad Dressing & Slaw
- 131. Ginger Miso Dressing & Sauce
- 131. Greek Yogurt Dressing & Marinade
- 132. Lemon Pepper Spread & Dressing
- 132. Creamy Ranch Dressing
- 132. Sweet Lemongrass Dressing
- 133. Taco Dressing
- 133. Tartar Sauce

Vegan, Gluten-Free, Grain Friendly

Bar-B-Que Sauce GF-Vegan

Whisk together in crockpot and cook on low for two hours
- ⅓ cup peanut oil
- 1 *Canna Bar-B-Que Spice Blend*
- ¾ teaspoon salt
- ¼ teaspoon pepper
- 4 tablespoons green onion, chopped
- 2 tablespoons lime juice

Add and continue cooking on low for two hours, covered
- 2 tablespoons raw apple cider vinegar
- 2 tablespoons Worcestershire sauce
- 2 tablespoons liquid amino or soy sauce
- 2 tablespoons honey

Remove lid to thicken, add water if too thick

Add
- ¼ teaspoon ginger, ground
- ½ cup pineapple, crushed
- ¾ cup tomato paste

Whisk-Whisk-Whisk

Chick Pea Croutons GF-Vegan

Shake in a bag, spread out on a cookie sheet
- 1 can chick peas, drained and dried
- 1 tablespoon + 1 teaspoon olive oil
- 1 *Canna Lemon Pepper Spice Blend*

Bake at 400°F for 30 minutes, shake once

Cocktail Sauce GF-Vegan

Sauté on low to medium heat for 10 minutes
- 2 tablespoons olive oil
- 1 *Canna Lemon Pepper Spice Blend*
- ¼ teaspoon salt

Blend in
- ¾ cup tomato paste
- ¼ cup tomato juice
- 4 tablespoons horseradish sauce
- ¼ cup lemon juice
- 1 tablespoon stevia

Garlic Thai Sauce GF-Vegan

Stir and simmer for 10 minutes on low
- 2 tablespoons peanut oil
- 1 *Canna Thai Spice Blend*
- 1 hot chili (Ch.3, pg. 73), diced
- ⅓ cup raw apple cider vinegar
- 12 garlic cloves, minced
- ¼ teaspoon salt
- ¼ cup stevia
- ¼ cup water

Whisk in
- 1½ teaspoons xanthan gum (GF optional)

Add and bring to a boil
- 1 teaspoon water
- 4 additional garlic cloves, minced

Puree and serve at room temperature.

Ginger Sesame Dressing GF-Vegan

Whisk
        ½ cup water
        ¼ cup liquid amino or soy sauce
        2 tablespoons xanthan gum (GF optional)
Microwave until boiling (approx. 30 sec), stir. Microwave another 30 seconds and stir. Cool in refrigerator
Slowly whisk into cooled liquid
        ¼ cup raw apple cider vinegar
        2¼ teaspoons stevia
        ½ cup *Canna* Sesame Infused Oil (Ch.2, pg.32)

Horseradish Chili Sauce GF-Vegan

Sauté on medium for 5 minutes
        3 tablespoons *Canna* Chili Oil (Ch.2, pgs.32)
        1 *Canna Chili Spice Blend*
        2 cups red onion, finely chopped
        1 teaspoon Tabasco
        1½ teaspoons salt
        ½ teaspoon pepper
Add then simmer for 5 minutes
        ¼ cup raw apple cider vinegar
        1 tablespoon Worcestershire sauce
        2 cups plum or Italian tomatoes with juice
After simmer, crush tomatoes
Remove from heat then add
        2 tablespoons horseradish
Blend with immersion blender and serve with meat or pasta

Hummus GF-Vegan

Sauté on medium for 15 minutes
> 3 tablespoons olive oil
> 1 *Canna Greek Island Spice Blend*
> ¼ teaspoon salt

Add, puree until smooth
> 4 garlic cloves
> 1½ cups chickpeas
> juice of 2 lemons

Roasted Tomato Hummus GF-Vegan

Prepare Roasted Tomatoes (Ch.9, pg.250)
Clean the soft cooked tomato meat from the skin and mash, set aside

Sauté for 15 minutes
> 3 tablespoons olive oil
> 1 *Greek Island Spice Blend*
> 1½ cups chickpeas
> 4 garlic cloves crushed
> juice of 2 lemons

Add & puree   tomatoes

Jamaican Mustard GF-Vegan almost fat free

Heat for 15 minutes
> 1 tablespoon olive oil
> 1 *Canna Jamaica Jerk Spice Blend*

Mix in, blend well
> 6 tablespoons prepared mustard
> Salt and pepper to taste

Jerk Sauce GF-Vegan

Make ahead and refrigerate
Sauté
    3 tablespoons olive oil
    1 *Canna Jamaican Jerk Spice Blend*
    ¾ teaspoon salt
    ¼ teaspoon pepper
    2 tablespoons onion, diced

Add and simmer one hour
    1 cup tomato sauce
    1 tomato paste, canned
    4 tablespoons stevia
    ½ cup + 1 tablespoon apple cider vinegar
    ¼ cup molasses
    2 tablespoons Worcestershire sauce

Kiwi Compote GF-Vegan

Pulse in blender or food processor to a coarse texture
    5 kiwis, peeled

Place in sauce pan
    ½ cup *Canna* Golden Gin Raisins (pg. 143)
    1 *Canna Fruit Pie Spice Blend*
    2 tablespoons coconut oil
    3 tablespoons honey

Simmer and stir on medium until thickened, 12-14 minutes. Chill and serve over cottage cheese, fish or chicken.

Lemon Pepper Dressing & Marinade GF-Vegan

Mix and heat for 15 minutes
- 2 tablespoons olive oil
- 1 *Canna Lemon Pepper Spice Blend*
- 2 tablespoons miso

Add and whisk
- 2 tablespoons raw apple cider vinegar
- 1 tablespoon Dijon mustard
- 2 tablespoons honey
- Salt to taste

Lemon Dressing GF-Vegan

Whisk
- ½ cup olive oil
- 1 *Canna Italian Spice Blend*
- ¾ teaspoon salt
- ¼ teaspoon pepper

Bring to a soft boil, simmer 20 minutes, set aside to cool

Combine in a separate small bowl
- 1 teaspoon lemon juice
- ½ cup raw apple cider vinegar
- ½ teaspoon lemon zest

Gradually whisk in seasoned oil until slightly thickened. Keep in airtight container for up to 1 week.

Lemongrass Salad Dressing GF-Vegan

Shake until dissolved
- 3 teaspoons stevia
- 4 tablespoons lemon juice
- 4 tablespoons lime juice

Add and shake
- 4 tablespoons mint leaves, chopped
- 1 cup *Canna Thai Spice Oil* (Ch.2, pg.32)
- ½ cup raw apple cider vinegar
- Salt and pepper to taste

Cover and store for up to three weeks in refrigerator

Mustard Dill Salad Dressing GF-Vegan-Low Calorie

Shake together, let rest for 24 hours at room temperature
- ½ cup olive oil
- (For fewer calories replace ¼ cup oil with water)
- 1 *Canna Pickling Spice Blend,* ground
- ¼ cup raw apple cider vinegar
- ¾ cup water
- 1 tablespoon yellow mustard

Mango Marinade, Salsa & Tenderizer GF-Vegan

Heat on low to medium heat for 10 minutes
- 3 tablespoons olive oil
- 1 *Canna Jamaica Jerk Spice Blend*
- 1 hot pepper, minced (Ch.3, pg.73)
- 1 mango, mashed
- ½ cup pineapple, minced

Add
- 3 tablespoons apple cider vinegar
- Salt and pepper to taste

Great for marinating the toughest meat and over poultry and fish; makes a great salsa.

Soy Mushroom Sauce GF-Vegan

Over medium to high heat whisk together for 8 minutes
> 2½ cups soy milk, plain, unsweetened
> ½ cup water
> ½ cup raw pistachios, soaked 2 hours, drained
> 2 tablespoons nutritional yeast
> 3 tablespoons oat flour

Add to sauce base, whisk and simmer for 10 minutes on low
> 1 tablespoons *Canna* Mushroom Oil (Ch.2, pgs.31-32)
> 1 *Canna Poultry Spice Blend*
> 1 teaspoon onion salt
> ¼ teaspoon pepper
> ¾ teaspoon salt

Grilled Red Onions GF-Vegan

Slice, coat and grill
> 3 red onions into large rings, held together with toothpicks
> 1 *Canna* Lemon Pepper Olive Oil (Ch.2, pgs.31-32)

Serve with more drizzled oil, salt, and another drizzle of raw apple cider vinegar.

Crispy Sage Onions GF-Vegan

Shake together
> 4 large onions thinly sliced
> 1 *Canna Poultry Spice Blend*
> 2 tablespoons coconut oil, room temperature

Heat in large pot over medium high heat 1 cup of coconut oil.
Add 3 handfuls of onions, a little at a time, to keep onions from sticking. Stir to keep loose. When dark golden brown, remove to a paper towel to drain and add another batch.

Fried Savory Onions GF-Vegan

Combine and toss
> 1 *Canna Savory Beef Spice Blend*
> 2 onions, large, thinly sliced
> Salt and pepper to taste

Fry onions in small batches in 1 inch of hot peanut oil, keep separated and remove to a towel.

NOTES

Quick & Easy Pizza Sauce GF-Vegan

Bring to a boil, cover and simmer 30 minutes
- 2 tablespoons olive oil
- 1 *Canna Italian Spice Blend*
- ¾ teaspoon salt
- ¼ teaspoon pepper
- 1-16-ounce tomato sauce, canned

Use fresh or freeze. Great on anything, eggs, rice, pasta and zucchini noodles

Pizza Sauce GF-Vegan

Sauté until onions are soft and browned
- 4 tablespoons olive oil
- 1 *Canna Italian Spice Blend*
- 4 garlic cloves, chopped
- ¼ teaspoon pepper
- ¾ teaspoon salt
- 1 onion, diced

Add
- 8 fresh Roma or Italian style tomatoes, chopped
- 1 cup tomato sauce

Bring to boil then simmer on low 1-4 hours depending on your taste or desired thickness, adjust with tomato juice. Great on anything! Eggs, rice, pasta and zucchini noodles

Rum or Gin Raisin Nut Sauce GF Vegan

Pour over bananas, pineapple, yogurt, sweet potatoes or lamb
Sauté for 15 minutes
- 4 tablespoons coconut oil
- 1 *Canna Spicy Jelly Spice Blend*

Add and continue to reduce for 5-10 minutes
- 1 cup apple juice
- 2 tablespoons xanthan

Add in
- ¼ cup *Canna* Rum or Gin (pg. 142)
- ¾ cup *Canna* Golden Gin or Rum Raisins (pg. 143)
- 1 cup pecans, chopped

Black Bean Jerk Salsa GF-Vegan

Heat on low to medium for 15 minutes then remove from heat
        ¼ cup olive oil
        1 *Canna Jamaican Jerk Spice Blend*
        ¼ teaspoon pepper
        ¾ teaspoon salt
Add   2 tablespoons raw apple cider vinegar
        1 can black beans, drained
        1 hot chili, diced (Ch.3, pg.73)
        1 green bell pepper, diced
        ½ cup red onion, diced
        1 can diced tomatoes, drained, reserving juice
        2 tablespoons of reserved tomato juice

Cucumber Salsa GF-Vegan

Heat on low to medium for 15 minutes, remove from heat
        3 tablespoons olive oil
        1 *Canna Lemon Pepper Spice Blend*
        ¾ teaspoon salt
Add   1 jalapeño, minced
        ¼ cup mint, chopped
        ½ cup red onion, diced
        ¼ cup cilantro, chopped
        2 tablespoons lime juice
        2 cucumbers, peeled and diced
        2 tablespoons raw apple cider vinegar
Mix together and chill for 1 hour.

Chunky Taco Salsa GF-Vegan

Heat on low to medium for 15 minutes then chill for at least 1 hour
        1 tablespoon olive oil
        1 *Canna Taco Spice Blend*
        ¾ teaspoon salt
Add   4 medium tomatoes chopped into ¼ in pieces
        1 cup red onion, minced
        6 red radishes, sliced
        2 cups cilantro, chopped
        2 tablespoons fresh lemon juice

Hot Pepper Salsa GF-Vegan

Dice   1 hot green pepper (Ch. 3, pg.73)
        1 hot red pepper (Ch. 3, pg.73)
        ½ pineapple
        ½ red onion
        ½ mango
        ½ papaya
        1 kiwi
Toss with 1 tablespoon *Canna* Honey (Ch.2, pg.31)
        2 tablespoons *Canna* Lemon Pepper Dressing (Ch.5, pg.109)

Spaghetti Sauce GF-Vegan

Sauté	4 tablespoons olive oil
	1 *Canna Italian Spice Blend*
	1 hot pepper minced, (Ch.3, pg.73)
	1 onion, diced
Add	1 28 ounces tomatoes, diced, canned
	1 cup Kalamata olives, sliced
	¼ cup capers, drained
Stir in	2 tablespoons raw apple cider vinegar
	1 tablespoon stevia
	¼ teaspoon pepper
	½ teaspoon salt

Simmer for 30 minutes or longer until you reach the desired consistency.

Tahini Dressing GF-Vegan

Heat on low to medium for 15 minutes, remove from heat
- 1 *Canna Chili Spice Blend*
- 3 tablespoons tahini
- ¼ teaspoon pepper
- ¾ teaspoon salt

Add & whisk
- ¼ cup water
- 1 teaspoon stevia
- 1 tablespoon lime juice
- 3 green onions, minced
- 1 tablespoon maple syrup
- ¼ cup liquid amino or soy sauce
- 1 tablespoon raw apple cider vinegar

Tomato Vinaigrette & Marinade GF-Vegan

Heat on low to medium for 10 minutes
> ½ cup olive oil
> 1 *Canna Italian Spice Blend*
> ¼ teaspoon pepper
> ¾ teaspoon salt

Add and whisk together
> 1 tablespoon maple syrup
> 1 tablespoon Dijon mustard
> 2 tablespoons raw apple cider vinegar

Refrigerate for up to 4 weeks.

Italian Red Wine Dressing GF-Vegan

Whisk and bring to a soft boil, simmer for 20 minutes, cool
> ½ cup olive oil
> 1 *Canna Italian Spice Blend*
> ¼ teaspoon pepper
> ¾ teaspoon salt

In a separate small bowl, whisk together
> ½ cup raw apple cider vinegar
> ½ teaspoon lemon juice
> ½ cup red wine

Combine with cooled *Canna* Italian Olive Oil and blend.
Keep in airtight container for up to 1 week.

White Wine Dressing GF-Vegan

Combine and marinate for 24 hours
> ½ cup olive oil
> 1 *Canna Chinese Five Spice Blend*
> 1 hot pepper minced (Ch.3, pg.73)
> ¼ cup raw apple cider vinegar
> 1 tablespoon honey
> ¼ teaspoon pepper
> ¾ teaspoon salt
> ½ cup white wine
> ½ cup water

Shake, shake, shake!

NOTES

Creamy Cooking Basics

Cream Skillet Sauté GF

Sauté meat of your choice, set aside. Scrape down the sides of the skillet, add and whisk over medium heat
> 3 tablespoons butter
> 1 *Canna Spice Blend* of your choice

Add and whisk 1 cup heavy cream
Heat to soft bubble, reduce heat
Add and simmer for 5 minutes while whisking
> ¾ cup salsa

Serve over sautéed meat

Basic Roux GF

Whisk 3 minutes over medium heat
> 3 tablespoons butter
> 1 *Canna Italian Spice Blend*
> 3 tablespoons xanthan gum (GF optional)
> ¼ teaspoon pepper
> ¾ teaspoon salt

Add, whisk and simmer until desired thickness
> 1 cup heavy cream

Coconut Cream GF

Mix, heat and simmer for 15 minutes
> 1 cup coconut milk
> 1 cup heavy cream
> 1 teaspoon vanilla

Use ½ cup in shakes, sauces and baking. Refrigerate the unused portion.

Spiced Cream GF

Whisk, heat and simmer for 15 minutes
> 1 cup heavy cream
> 1 cup skim milk
> 1 *Canna Spicy Jelly Spice Blend*

Use in recipes calling for cream and refrigerate the unused portion.

Milk GF

Mix, heat and simmer for 15 minutes
> 1 cup heavy cream
> 1 *Canna Fruit Pie Spice Blend*
> 1 cup water
> 1 cup skim milk

Use in recipes calling for milk and refrigerate the unused portion.

Coffee and Tea Creamer GF - 3 tablespoons =1 serving

Whisk, heat and simmer for 15 minutes
> 1 cup heavy cream
> 1 cup skim milk
> 1 *Canna Fruit Pie Spice Blend*
> 3 teaspoons cannabis, optional

Use in small amounts due to the high content of cannabis. Adjust the added cannabis for personal taste and desired results.

Creamy Dressings & Toppings

Blue Cheese Dressing GF

Whisk together
- ¼ cup water
- ½ cup yogurt, plain
- ¼ cup olive oil
- ½ cup mayonnaise
- 1 tablespoon stevia
- ¼ cup raw apple cider vinegar
- 1 *Canna Lemon Pepper Spice Blend*

Add 4 ounces crumbled blue cheese

Make 24-48 hours in advance to set

Butter Garlic Cream Sauce

Sauté on low for 10 minutes
  ¼ cup butter, unsalted
  1 *Canna Lemon Pepper Spice Blend*
Add and sauté for an additional 3 minutes
  1 clove garlic, minced
Add ½ cup heavy cream
  ¼ cup chicken broth
  4 teaspoons xanthan gum (GF optional)
  Salt and pepper to taste
Whisk & simmer until desired thickness

Creamy Cesar Dressing

Sauté for 10 minutes
  4 tablespoons olive oil
  1 *Canna Greek Island Spice Blend*
  4 garlic cloves, smashed
Let mixture cool, removing cloves after cooling
Whisk into oil ½ cup yogurt
  ½ cup mayonnaise
  ½ cup heavy cream
  Salt and pepper to taste

Italian Bake & Fry Blend

Shake it and bake it! Use for chicken fried steak, fish and chips and sweet potato fries. Coat in spray oil, beaten eggs, water or milk then shake, bake & enjoy!

Pulse for 30 seconds in a blender or food processor
- 1 *Canna Italian Spice Blend*
- 1 cup onions, dehydrated
- 1 teaspoon garlic, minced
- ½ teaspoon pepper
- 1 teaspoon salt

Add and pulse for 10 seconds
- 1 cup Parmesan cheese, shredded

Can be refrigerated up to 2 weeks in a sealed container

NOTES

Jamaican Butter Cream Sauce GF

Sauté on low for 10 minutes
       ¼ cup butter, unsalted
       1 *Canna Jamaican Jerk Spice Blend*
Add and sauté for an additional 3 minutes
       1 clove garlic, minced
Add   ¼ cup chicken broth
       ½ cup heavy cream
       2 tablespoons xanthan gum (GF optional)
       ½ cup hot salsa
       Salt and pepper to taste
Wisk & simmer until desired thickness

Cheese Mushroom Sauce GF

Sauté on low for 15 minutes
       2 tablespoons butter, unsalted or ghee
       1 *Canna Savory Beef Spice Blend*
       3 cups mushrooms, cleaned, trimmed and sliced
Add   ½ cup heavy cream
       ½ cup skim milk
Bring to a soft boil, remove from heat
Add and puree all ingredients together
       ½ cup fresh Parmesan cheese, grated
       ½ cup goat cheese, grated
       Pepper to taste

Pepper Cole Slaw Dressing GF

Mix together then let sit for 15 minutes
       1 *Canna Lemon Pepper Spice Blend*
       ¾ cup yogurt
       ½ cup mayonnaise
       2 tablespoons stevia
       1 teaspoon lemon juice
       1 tablespoon raw apple cider
       Salt and pepper to taste

Bitter Sweet Cream Sauce GF Dip and spread

Heat on medium for 10 minutes, set aside to cool
    ¼ cup heavy cream
    1 *Canna Fruit Pie Spice Blend*
Beat   1 cup heavy cream until firm peaks form
Add in and beat cooled Spiced Cream
Add   4 teaspoons stevia
    1 teaspoon almond extract
Fold in   ½ cup Greek yogurt

Cheese Sauce GF

Sauté for 10 minutes, cool
    2 tablespoons butter or ghee
    1 *Canna Italian Spice Blend*
Add to Canna butter
    ½ cup heavy cream
    1 teaspoon garlic, minced
Whisk on medium heat until it begins to boil
Add   1 cup cheese, ¼ cup at a time while whisking
    (Parmesan, Goat, Ricotta, Gouda, Jack, Havarti, Colby or Cheddar)

Curry Dressing & Marinade GF

Shake   ½ cup yogurt
    ¾ cup water
    1 teaspoon stevia
    ½ cup peanut oil
    1 *Canna Curry Spice Blend*
    ¼ cup raw apple cider vinegar
    1 tablespoon peanut butter microwaved to soften
    Salt and pepper to taste
Make a day ahead for *Canna*bis action. Refrigerate up to 3 weeks.
For marinade, add ½ cup red wine and remove the yogurt

Dill Sauce GF

Heat on low to medium for 15 minutes
    ¼ cup heavy cream
    1 *Canna Greek Island Spice Blend*
    1 tablespoon fresh dill
    ½ teaspoon garlic salt
Add   1 tablespoon dill pickle, minced
    ¼ cup mayonnaise
    ¼ cup yogurt
    Salt and pepper to taste
Finish with dill sprigs

Goat Cheese Sprinkles GF

Combine   1 cup *Canna* Italian Olive Oil (Ch.2, Pg.32)
    1 cup goat cheese, crumbled
Leave at room temperature for 6 hours and then chill

Greek Dressing & Marinade GF

Shake together
    ½ cup olive oil
    1 *Canna Greek Island Spice Blend*
    ¼ cup raw apple cider vinegar
    2 tablespoons lemon juice
    ½ cup Greek yogurt
    1 teaspoon stevia
    Salt and pepper to taste
For marinade, add ½ cup red wine and remove the yogurt

Creamy Lemon Pepper Dressing GF

Mix together and heat on low to medium for 15 minutes
    2 tablespoons olive oil
    1 *Canna Lemon Pepper Spice Blend*
    2 tablespoons miso
Add and whisk together
    2 tablespoons raw apple cider vinegar
    1 tablespoon Dijon mustard
    2 tablespoons honey
    ¼ cup yogurt
    Salt and pepper to taste

Fresh Lime Dressing GF

Puree	1½ cups scallions or green onions, chopped
Add	½ cup *Canna* Lemon Mayonnaise (below)
	juice of 1 lime
	Salt and pepper to taste

Curry or Lemon Mayonnaise

Sauté on low to medium heat for 10 minutes, cool
    3 tablespoons coconut oil
    1 *Canna Curry* or *Canna Lemon Pepper Spice Blend*
    1 inch ginger, minced
Whisk in   1 cup mayonnaise

Savory Mayonnaise GF

Sauté on low to medium heat for 10 minutes, cool
    3 tablespoons butter
    1 *Canna Savory Beef Spice Blend*
    1 hot pepper, minced (Ch.3, pg.73)
Whisk in   1 cup mayonnaise

Spicy Mayonnaise Butter Spread GF

Sauté on low to medium heat for 10 minutes, let cool
        3 tablespoons butter
        1 *Canna Chili Spice Blend*
        1 hot pepper, minced (Ch.3, pg.73)
Whisk in   1 cup mayonnaise
        Salt and pepper to taste

Oven Fried Onions GF

Combine and toss
        2 tablespoons bran
        2 large onions, thinly sliced
        1 *Canna Savory Beef Spice Blend*
Whisk   1 egg white, and toss in onion mix
Spread out in a single layer on a parchment lined baking sheet and bake at 350°F for 25 minutes or until very golden brown, turning once. Remove and turn again. Perfect condiment for salad, fish, meat & legumes.

Yogurt Dressings

Chili Yogurt Salad Dressing & Marinade GF

Heat on low to medium for 15 minutes, cool
        ½ cup olive oil
        1 *Canna Chili Spice Blend*
In shaker jar add to *Canna Chili Oil*
        ¼ cup raw apple cider vinegar
        1 teaspoon stevia
        ½ cup yogurt
        ¼ cup water
        Salt and pepper to taste
Mix and chill for 1 hour. For marinade, add ½ cup red wine and omit the yogurt. Refrigerate up to 3 weeks.

NOTES

Chinese Yogurt Salad Dressing & Slaw GF

Whisk
- 1 tablespoon *Canna* Raw Apple Cider Vinegar (Pg.32)
- ½ cup *Canna* Lemon Pepper Mayonnaise (Ch.5, pg.128)
- 1 shake Tabasco sauce
- juice of 1 lemon
- 3 teaspoons stevia
- ¼ teaspoon pepper
- ¾ teaspoon salt
- ½ cup yogurt

Set aside for 1 or more hours (longer is better)

Add & toss
- 1 fennel bulb, thinly sliced
- 4 cups red or purple cabbage, shredded

Ginger Miso Yogurt Dressing & Sauce GF

Shake together. Refrigerate for up to 3 weeks.
- ¾ cup water
- ½ cup yogurt
- ½ cup peanut oil
- 2 tablespoons miso paste
- ½ teaspoon ginger, ground
- ¼ cup raw apple cider vinegar
- ½ teaspoon ginger, fresh, grated
- 1 *Canna Chinese Five Spice Blend*
- Salt and pepper to taste

Greek Yogurt Dressing & Marinade GF

Heat on low to medium heat for 15 minutes, cool
- ½ cup olive oil
- 1 *Canna Greek Island Spice Blend*

In a shaker, add to cooled oil and shake
- ½ cup Greek yogurt
- ¼ cup raw apple cider vinegar
- 1 teaspoon stevia
- 2 tablespoons lemon juice
- Salt and pepper to taste

For marinade, add ½ cup red wine and omit the yogurt.

Lemon Pepper Yogurt Spread & Dressing GF

Sauté on low to medium heat for 10 minutes, cool
- 2 tablespoons olive oil (for dressing double)
- 1 *Canna Lemon Pepper Spice Blend*

Mix in
- 3 tablespoons raw apple cider vinegar
- 3 tablespoons honey
- ½ cup Greek yogurt
- ½ cup mayonnaise
- Salt to taste

Creamy Ranch Yogurt Dressing GF

Sauté on low to medium heat for 15 minutes, cool
- ½ cup olive oil
- 1 *Canna Lemon Pepper Spice Blend*

Whisk in
- ¼ cup raw apple cider vinegar
- ½ cup yogurt, plain
- 1 tablespoon stevia
- ¼ cup water
- Salt and pepper to taste

Sweet Lemongrass Yogurt Dressing GF

Puree
- 1 peeled apple, chopped
- ¼ cup coconut

Add and mix
- 4 tablespoons yogurt
- 4 tablespoons lime juice
- ½ cup raw apple cider vinegar
- 4 tablespoons mint leaves, chopped
- 1 cup *Canna* Thai Spice Blend Oil (Ch.2, pg.32)
- 4 tablespoons lemon juice
- 6 teaspoons stevia, dissolved in the lemon juice
- Salt and pepper to taste

Taco Yogurt Dressing GF

Sauté on low to medium heat for 15 minutes, cool
    ½ cup olive oil
    1 *Canna Taco Spice Blend*
Whisk in   ½ cup yogurt
    1 teaspoon stevia
    ¼ cup tomato juice
    ¼ cup raw apple cider vinegar
    Salt and pepper to taste
For marinade, add ½ cup red wine and remove the yogurt

Tartar Sauce GF

Sauté on low to medium heat for 15 minutes, cool
    2 tablespoons olive oil
    1 *Canna Thai Spice Blend*
Blend into spiced oil
    ½ cup yogurt
    1 teaspoon stevia
    ½ cup mayonnaise
    ½ cup dill pickle relish
    Salt and pepper to taste
Adjust consistency with lemon juice.
Let stand 4 hours at room temperature. Keeps up to 2 weeks in refrigerator.

NOTES

Chapter 6: Hydration & Libations

COFFEE & CHOCOLATE
138. Chocolate Milk
138. Whey Dark Cherry Chocolate
138. Love Bud Milk
139. Pot of Iced or Hot Mocha
139. Coffee and Tea Creamer
139. Cafe Mocha

COCKTAIL HELPERS
140. Ginger Simple Syrup
140. Simple Syrup

141. ALCOHOL INFUSIONS

SPECIALTY COCKTAILS
142. Spiced Star Bourbon
142. Spicy Bourbon Pie
142. Lemongrass Gin
142. Kahlua
142. Star Orange Liquor
142. Spiced Dark Rum
142. Gingered Light Rum
142. Spicy Tequila
143. Star Tequila
143. Gingered Vodka
143. Lemon Pepper Vodka
143. Saffron Vodka
143. Spiced Star Whisky
143. Spicy Whisky Pie
143. Golden Gin or Rum Raisins

GREEN JUICES & SMOOTHIES
146. Collard Green Blends
146. Digestion Detox
147. Dandelion Green Blends
147. Green Energy Juice
147. Green Love Potion
148. Green Power Smoothie
148. Kale Blends
149. Spinach Blends
149. Swiss chard Blends
150. Watercress Blends

FRUIT & VEGETABLE JUICES AND SMOOTHIES
152. Anti-inflammatory Detox
152. Coconut Almond Smoothie
152. Coconut Cream
152. Frozen Lime Coconut
152. Cucumber Mint
153. Energy Tea Smoothie
153. Fiber Fennel Smoothie
153. Fiber Pumpkin Detox
153. Ginger Lemonade
153. Kiwi Strawberry
154. Frozen Mango Peach
154. Orange Mango Creamsicle
154. Melon Love Juice
154. Pineapple Mint
154. Raspberry Rose Buds
155. Strawberry Passion Juice
155. Strawberries & Cream
155. Strawberry Yogurt Smoothie
155. Water Hydro Drinks
157. Watermelon Excitement
157. Watermelon Smoothie
157. Watermelon Weight Loss

TEA
158. Black tea
158. Green Tea
158. White Tea

Coffee & Chocolate

Chocolate Milk (hot-cold-iced)

(For fewer calories, use equal parts water to cream)
Whisk, heat over low for 10 minutes
> 3 cups heavy cream
> 1 cup water
> 1 Canna Fruit Pie Spice Blend

Add, stir to dissolve
> ½ cup dark baking chocolate
> 4 teaspoons stevia

Heat and stir for 20 minutes, chill
Frosty: blend with 1-2 cups Canna Tea ice cubes (Ch.2, pg.27)

Whey Dark Cherry Chocolate Smoothie

This nutritious treat is my personal favorite, but beware of the calories.

Blend
> 1 packet acai smoothie packet (broken into pieces)
> ½ cup water
> 1 scoop whey protein
> 1 cup dark red cherries, frozen
> ½ banana or yogurt and stevia
> ¾ cup Canna Cream (Ch.5, pg.139)
> 2 tablespoons flax seed, freshly ground
> 1 tablespoon dark chocolate, ground

Love Buds Milk

Individual serving size 3 tablespoons
Heat and whisk
> ½ cup heavy cream
> 1 Canna Fruit Pie Spice Blend
> 3 teaspoons cannabis

Add and simmer for 15 minutes, strain
> 1 ½ cup skim milk

Refrigerate for up to 1 week.

Pot of Iced or Hot Canna Mocha

Brew   8 cups coffee (regular, decaf or ½ and ½)
In a small sauce pan bring to a soft boil
        2 cups heavy cream (or ½ cream and ½ water)
        1 *Canna Fruit Pie Spice Blend*
        2 teaspoons cannabis
Reduce heat immediately to low; simmer for 10 minutes and continue to stir.
Whisk in   1 teaspoon vanilla extract
        4 tablespoons cocoa, unsweetened
        5 teaspoons stevia
Serve hot or cool and serve over Ice or even better, blend with 1 cup of ice for a great frosty.

Coffee and Tea Creamer

Individual serving size, 3 tablespoons
Use in small amounts due to the higher content of cannabis.
Adjust the added cannabis for personal taste and results.

Heat, whisk and simmer for 15 minutes, strain and serve
        2 cups heavy cream
        1 *Canna Fruit Pie Spice Blend*
        3 teaspoons cannabis
Refrigerate for up to one week

Cafe Mocha (hot-iced-frosty)

Stir together   1 cup *Canna* Chocolate Milk (Ch.5, pg.138)
        4 cups strong coffee, hot or cold
Top with Whipped Cream (Ch.10, pg.283) and coco sprinkles

Cocktail Helpers

Ginger Simple Syrup

Boil for 15 minutes: 1 tablespoon + 2 teaspoons stevia, ½ cup warm water, 1 *Canna Fruit Pie Spice Blend* and 1 teaspoon sliced ginger. Shake or stir. Store in the refrigerator for up to 3 weeks

Simple Syrup

Boil for 15 minutes: 3 ½ tablespoons stevia, ½ cup warm water, 1 *Canna Fruit Pie Spice Blend.* Shake or stir. Store in refrigerator for up to 3 weeks

See also:
Canna Tea and *Canna* Ice Cubes, pg. 27
Canna Milk and Cream, pg. 138-139
Canna Whip cream, pg. 283

Alcohol Infusions

Place 3-4 ounces of leaf, 2 ounces of sweet leaf or 1 ounce of buds in a cheese cloth baggie. Add to a quart of Everclear®, vodka, rum or gin. (Be aware that Everclear® is a much stronger proof alcohol.) Place in freezer, shaking 2 times daily for 5 days, or for 10 days if stored in a dark cool place. Strain and store in a sealed dark glass bottle.

Specialty Cocktails

Enjoy flavored alcohols by adding *Canna Spice Blends* before storing.
Place in freezer shaking 2 times a day for 5 days, or for 10 days if stored in a dark cool place. Strain and store in a sealed dark bottle.

Spiced Star Bourbon
1 pint bourbon + 2 *Canna Chinese Five Spice Blend*s

Spicy Bourbon Pie
1 pint bourbon + 2 *Canna Spicy Jelly Spice Blend*

Lemongrass Gin
1 pint gin + 2 *Canna Thai Spice Blend*s
4 lemongrass sprigs

Kahlua
1 pint Kahlua, 12 coffee beans + *2 Canna Spicy Jelly Spice Blends*

Star Orange Liquor
1 pint orange liquor + 2 *Canna Thai Spice Blends*
4 tablespoons dried orange rind

Spiced Dark Rum
1 pint dark rum + 2 *Canna Spicy Jelly Spice Blends*
1 orange peel

Gingered Light Rum
1 pint light rum + 2 *Canna Thai Spice Blend*s
4 tablespoons ginger, sliced

Spicy Tequila
1 pint tequila + 2 *Canna Taco Spice Blends*
2 tablespoons chilies, dried

Star Tequila
    1 pint tequila + 2 *Canna Chinese Five Spice Blends*
    12 cloves, whole

Gingered Vodka
    1 pint vodka + 2 *Canna Thai Spice Blend*s
    4 tablespoons ginger, sliced

Lemon Pepper Vodka
    1 pint vodka + 2 *Canna Lemon Pepper Spice Blends*
    1 tablespoon lemon peel

Saffron Vodka
    1 pint vodka + 2 *Canna French Spice Blend*
    1 tablespoon saffron threads

Spiced Star Whisky
    1 pint whisky + 2 *Canna Chinese Five Spice Blends*
    12 cloves, whole

Spicy Whisky Pie
    1 pint whisky + 2 *Canna Spicy Jelly Spice Blends*
    4 cinnamon sticks
    12 cloves, whole

Golden *Canna* Gin or Rum Raisins
    4 ounces gin or rum
    4 ounces golden raisins
    2 grams cannabis trim
    1 *Canna* Spicy Jelly Spice Blend

Store in refrigerator for up to 1 year. Use as a topping, snack and in other recipes. Some say it reduces the discomfort from arthritis.

NOTES

Green Juices and Smoothies

Add *Canna Green Power or Maca Happy Powder Blend* to all your favorite smoothies and juice. See the Food List for all the health benefits of this amazing *Green Powder*. Personalize with lemons, limes, stevia, honey, maple or dates.

Collard Green Blends

Puree   1 cup collard greens, 1 cup *Canna* Tea (Ch.2, pg.25-27)
½ cup pineapple, ½ cup red grapes
3 tablespoons acai or goji berries
1 tablespoon *Canna Green Power Powder*

Puree   2 cups collard greens, 1 date
3 tablespoons each: lime, lemon, grapefruit juice (including rind and zest)
1 tablespoon *Canna Green Power Powder*

Puree   2 cups collard greens
½ cup each: strawberries, blueberries, raspberries
3 tablespoons gogi or acai smoothie packet
1 tablespoon *Canna Green Power Powder*

Digestion Detox serves 2

Blend   2 cups *Canna* Dandelion Detox Tea (Ch.2, pg.25)
1 cup dandelion greens
½ cup each: fennel, celery, pears and pineapple
½ cup Greek yogurt
¼ cup kimchi
1 teaspoon stevia dates or honey
2 tablespoons *Canna Green Power Powder*

Dandelion Green Blends (use young tender leaves)

Puree
1 cup packed greens
2 cups *Canna* Dandelion Detox Tea (Ch.2, pg.25)
½ cup each: blueberries and pineapple
½ orange
1 tablespoon *Canna Green Power Powder*

Puree
1 cup packed greens
2 cups *Canna* Dandelion Detox Tea (Ch.2, pg.25)
½ cup each: cantaloupe, papaya, cottage cheese
1 tablespoon *Canna Green Power Powder*

Puree
1 cup packed greens
2 cups *Canna* Dandelion Detox Tea (Ch.2, pg.25)
½ avocado, 3 tablespoons lemon juice, ½ mango, ½ papaya
1 tablespoon *Canna Green Power Powder*

Green Energy Juice serves 2

Puree
4 kiwis, peeled
2 cups dandelion greens
2 teaspoons stevia or ground dates
3 cups *Canna* Green Energy Tea (Ch.2, pg.26)
2 tablespoons *Canna Green Power Powder*

Green Love Potion serves 2

Blend
2 cups *Canna Jasmine Bud Tea* (Ch.2, pg.27)
1 cup watermelon, cubed
1 kiwi, peeled
1 cup strawberries, hulled
1 tablespoon *Canna Green Powder*
1 tablespoon flax seed ground
1 tablespoon *Canna Maca Happy Powder*
1 teaspoon stevia, honey, maple syrup or dates

Green Power Smoothie serves 2

Blend
- 1 cup *Canna Saffron Ginger Memory Tea* (Ch.2, pg.27)
- 1 cup nori or acai juice
- 1 cup blueberries
- juice of 1 lime
- 1 teaspoon flax seed, ground
- 1 cup watercress greens
- ½ cup Greek yogurt
- 1 tablespoon *Canna Green Power Powder*
- 2 teaspoons stevia, adjust to taste

Add tea to adjust for thickness

Kale Blends

Puree
- 1 cup kale, 3 cups *Canna* Tea ice cubes (Ch.2, pg.27)
- ½ cup each: avocado, red grapes, watermelon
- 1 tablespoon *Canna Green Power Powder*

Puree
- 1 cup kale, 3 cups *Canna* Tea ice cubes
- ½ apple, ½ cup blueberries, 1 fig, 3 tablespoons acai or gogi berries
- 1 tablespoon *Canna Green Power Powder*

Puree
- 1 cup kale, 3 cups *Canna* Tea ice cubes
- ½ cup each: avocado, cucumber and cantaloupe
- ¼ cup mint
- 1 tablespoon *Canna Green Power Powder*

Spinach Blends serves 2

Puree 1 cup spinach, 3 cups *Canna* Tea ice cubes (Ch.2, pg.27)
½ cup each: honeydew, strawberries, blueberries
1 tablespoon *Canna Green Power Powder*

Puree 1 cup spinach, 3 cups *Canna* Tea ice cubes
½ cup each: apple, pear, pineapple, blueberries, strawberries
1 tablespoon *Canna Green Power Powder*

Puree 1 cup spinach, 3 cups *Canna* Tea ice cubes
½ cup each: avocado, mango and strawberries
3 tablespoons acai or gogi berries
1 tablespoon *Canna Green Power Powder*

Swiss Chard Blends serves 2

Puree 1 cup Swiss chard, 3 cups *Canna* Tea ice cubes
½ apple, ½ cup blueberries, ½ cup pineapple, 3 tablespoons acai or goji berries
1 tablespoon *Canna Green Power Powder*

Puree 1 cup Swiss chard, 3 cups *Canna* Tea ice cubes
½ mango and ½ cup strawberries
1 kiwi, peeled and 3 tablespoons acai or gogi berries
1 tablespoon *Canna Green Power Powder*

Watercress Blends serves 2

Puree   1 cup watercress, 3 cups *Canna* Tea ice cubes (Ch.2, pg.27)
        ½ peach, ½ cup honeydew and ½ cup berries
        2 tablespoons *Canna Green Power Powder*

Puree   1 cup watercress, 3 cups *Canna* Tea ice cubes
        ½ avocado, ½ cup raspberries and ½ orange
        2 tablespoons *Canna Green Power Powder*

Puree   1 cup watercress, 3 cups *Canna* Tea ice cubes
        ½ cup each: red grapes, watermelon, broccoli
        3 tablespoons red beets, cooked
        2 tablespoons *Canna Green Power Powder*

Puree   1 cup watercress, 3 cups *Canna* Tea ice cubes
        ½ apple, ½ cup blueberries and ½ cup pineapple
        2 tablespoons *Canna Green Power Powder*

Puree   1 cup watercress, 3 cups *Canna* Tea ice cubes
        ½ inch ginger root, grated, 3 tablespoons lemon juice with zest, ½ pear and ½ avocado
        2 tablespoons *Canna Green Power Powder*

Puree   1 cup watercress, 3 cups *Canna* Tea ice cubes
        3 tablespoons each: avocado, berries
        1 inch ginger root, grated
        2 tablespoons *Canna Green Power Powder*

Fruit & Vegetable Juices & Smoothies

Adjust flavor with lemons, limes, stevia, honey, maple or dates. We love to add *Canna Green Power* or *Maca Happy Powder* to this group. When mixing fruits and vegetables, beware of certain combinations that may turn a murky color.

Anti-inflammatory Detox Juice

Blend ½ cup dark cherries
    ¼ cup fennel, chopped
    1 celery stalk, chopped
    1 lime, quartered with rind, seeds removed
    1 lemon, quartered with rind, seeds removed
    2 cups *Canna* Chai Tea (Ch.2, pg.25)

Coconut Almond Smoothie

Blend 1 cup coconut water
    1 teaspoon honey
    1 kale leaf, chopped
    1 cup *Canna* Tea ice cubes (Ch.2, pg.27)
    1 tablespoon coconut meat
    1 tablespoon coconut yogurt
    1 tablespoon *Canna* Almond Butter (Ch.2, pg.31)

Coconut Cream

Blend ¼ cup parsley
    1 teaspoon stevia
    1 cup *Canna* Tea ice cubes (Ch.2, pg.27)
    8 ounces coconut milk

Frozen Lime Coconut serves 6

Puree ¼ cup lime juice
    ¼ cup mint leaves, packed
    3 tablespoons stevia simple syrup
    2 (13 ounce) cans coconut milk, light
    4 cups *Canna* Rose Bud Tea ice cubes

Cucumber Mint

Blend 1 cucumber
    4 mint leaves, celery, cilantro (any or all)
    2 cups *Canna* French Saffron Tea (Ch.2, pg.27)

Energy Tea Smoothie

Blend   1 cup black tea, cooled
1 cup blueberries
½ cup peaches, sliced
5 *Canna* Tea ice cubes, (Ch.1, Pg.27)
5 ounces vanilla Greek yogurt, nonfat
Use 10 cubes with fresh fruit and 5 cubes with frozen fruit

Fiber Fennel Smoothie

Puree   1 pear, cubed
1 teaspoon honey
¼ cup fennel, chopped
4 celery stalks, chopped
1 teaspoon flax seeds, ground
1 tablespoon raw apple cider vinegar
1 cup *Canna* Detox Tea ice cubes (Ch.2, pg.25-27)

Fiber Pumpkin Detox serves 2

Blend   1 lemon, peeled, quartered, deseeded
1 teaspoon stevia
1 apple and 1 pear
½ cup pumpkin puree
1 tablespoon flax seed, ground
2 cup *Canna* Dandelion Detox Tea (Ch.2, pg.25)

Ginger Lemonade serves 2

Puree   4 lemons, peeled, quartered, deseeded
4 cups *Canna* Saffron Ginger Memory Tea (Ch.2, pg.27)
2 teaspoons stevia, honey or maple

Kiwi Strawberry serves 4

Blend   1 cup kale
¾ cup skim milk
1 cup strawberries, hulled
1 teaspoon ginger, ground
2 kiwi, peeled and chopped

4 cups *Canna* Tea ice cubes (Ch.1, Pg.27)

Frozen Mango Peach serves 6

Puree
½ orange
¼ cup lime juice
1 cup mango, cubed
4 cups peaches, frozen and sliced
3 tablespoons *Canna* Simple Syrup (Ch.6, pg.140)
4 cups *Canna* Mango Black Tea ice cubes (Ch.2, pg.25-27)

Orange Mango Creamsicle serves 2

Puree
1 teaspoon vanilla
1 mango, peeled and cubed
2 oranges, peeled and cubed
1 cup *Canna* Coconut Cream
1 cup *Canna* Orange Cinnamon Tea ice cubes

Melon Love Juice serves 4

Puree
1 lemon, peeled, quartered, deseeded
1 cup honeydew, cubed
1 cup cantaloupe, cubed
1 cup watermelon, cubed
3 cups *Canna* Jasmine Buds Tea (Ch.2, pg.27)
1 teaspoon stevia, honey or maple

Pineapple Mint

Puree
¼ cup mint
1 cup pineapple, cubed
1 cup *Canna* Hibiscus Ginger Lemon Tea ice cubes (Ch.2, Pg.26-27)

Raspberry Rose Buds serves 2

Puree
1 lemon, peeled, quartered, deseeded
1 cup raspberries
½ cup blueberries
1 tablespoon honey
3 cups *Canna* Red Rose Bud Tea (Ch.2, pg.26)

Strawberry Passion Juice serves 4

Puree
3 cups *Canna* White Passion Flower Tea (Ch.2, pg.26)
1 cup raspberries
1 cup strawberries, hulled
1 cup watermelon, cubed
1 teaspoon honey or stevia

Strawberries & Cream

Blend
2 cups strawberries, hulled
6 *Canna* Tea ice cubes (Ch.2, pg.27)
1½ cups Whipped Cream (Ch.10, pg.283)

Strawberry Yogurt Smoothie serves 2

Blend
½ cup nonfat milk
1½ cups strawberries, hulled
2 cups nonfat yogurt
2 teaspoons vanilla extract
¾ cup *Canna* Cream (Ch.5, pg.121)
2 tablespoons honey or 1 teaspoon stevia

Water Hydro Drinks

Keep your refrigerator stocked with these flavorful hydrations

- Water with Cucumber, celery and cilantro
- Water with Lemon-lime, ginger & stevia
- Water with ½-1 gram of saffron to 1 liter of water

Combine all ingredients in a pitcher and refrigerate for 12-24 hours to allow the water to infuse. Refill with water for up to 3-4 days before replacing the ingredients with fresh ones.

Watermelon Excitement serves 4

Puree 1 tablespoon stevia
     1 tablespoon lemon juice
     3 cups watermelon, cubed
     1 cup *Canna* French Saffron Tea (Ch.2, pg.27)

Watermelon Smoothie

Warm for 10 minutes over medium heat stirring often; cool.
     1 cup heavy cream
     2 tablespoons stevia
     1 *Canna Spicy Jelly Spice Blend*
Blend with 7 cups watermelon, cubed

Watermelon Weight Loss serves 4

Puree ½ cucumber, sliced
     ½ banana, sliced
     1 cup baby spinach
     1 celery stalk, chopped
     ½ cup pineapple, cubed
     1 cup watermelon, cubed
     6 ounces Greek yogurt, nonfat
     2 cups *Canna* Detox Tea ice cubes (Ch.2, pg.25-27)

Tea

See our Canna Tea list, Ch.2, pgs. 25-27

Black tea: an oxidized tea with half the caffeine of coffee, but more caffeine than green and white teas. Black tea is the leading tea for reducing LDL's (the bad form of cholesterol), the risk of stroke and heart disease and for building stronger blood vessels. Black tea is sometimes mistakenly called fermented, when it is actually oxidized.
See http://www.eliteabar.com/blogs/tea-education/7564628-tea-oxidation.

Green tea: the least-processed tea and the least oxidized. It is known for its medicinal powers, including: lowering the risk of Alzheimer's, artery disease, cancer, and blood clots. Green tea helps lower blood sugar and is beneficial in weight loss, relaxation, calming the nerves, and boosting one's mood.
See http://www.teavivre.com/info/how-to-process-green-tea/.

White tea: the super tea. White tea is barely processed, using tender baby leaves with buds that have not opened yet. It is then withered, or dried. Highest in antioxidants, polyphones and vitamins, white tea delivers the most healing properties with less caffeine than black or green tea.
See http://theteadetective.com/WhiteTeaProcessed.html.

NOTES

Chapter 7: Brunch with a Punch

BREAD
162. BRAN BREAD
162. BREAKFAST BLUEBERRY MUFFINS
163. SPICE CARROT BREAD
163. LEMON BUTTER CRUMBS
164. SPICY BRAN CRUMBS
164. ZUCCHINI BREAD

CREPES & PANCAKES
165. CREPES
165. RUM RAISIN NUT
166. PINEAPPLE
166. PUMPKIN

CRACKERS
168. ALMOND
168. QUICK BAR B QUE
168. TACO CHIPS
169. SWEET CINNAMON
169. QUICK BRAN
170. QUICK PB & J GRAHAM
170. FLAT BREAD
171. RYE

OATMEAL-ROLLED OATS
172. OATMEAL
172. HONEY NUT GRANOLA
173. CHOCOLATE CHIP COOKIE

DAIRY
174. SPICED FRUIT COTTAGE CHEESE
174. PEPPERED COTTAGE CHEESE
174. CHEESE TORTILLA CHIPS

EGGS
177. SALMON HASH BAKED EGGS
177. BOILED EGGS
177. CURRY DEVILED EGGS
178. EGG SALAD
178. DILL DEVILED EGGS
179. SARDINE DEVILED EGGS
180. CREPES (WHEAT FREE)
180. CHINESE FIVE
180. CURRY
180. ITALIAN
181. TACO
181. MUSHROOM & CHEESE SAUCE
181. STEAK & EGGS

FRIED EGGS
182. BACON SPINACH FRY
183. POACHED
184. SALMON & CREAM CHEESE
184. SPINACH & TOMATOES

QUICHE
185. QUICK & EASY LEMON CRUST
185. CHILI BRAN CRUST
186. PARMESAN KALE CRUST
186. SHRIMP, BROCCOLI & LEEK

SCRAMBLED
187. SOFT SCRAMBLE
187. AVOCADO

STEAMED
188. TOMATO & GOAT CHEESE

SALADS

FRUIT & VEGETABLE
190. AVOCADO GRAPEFRUIT SALAD
190. CUCUMBER SALAD
190. JICAMA STICKS
191. GRAPE BALLS
191. FRUIT SALAD
191. BAKED KALE CHIPS
192. KIMCHI
192. KIWI COMPOTE
192. FROZEN MANGO SLUSH
193. GRILLED PEACH & CHEESE SALAD
193. GIN RAISINS
193. WATERMELON, BLUEBERRY

PROTEIN SALAD
194. BACON & EGG SALAD
194. CURRY CHICKEN WRAP
195. CHICKEN WALDORF SALAD
195. COLESLAW
195. DANDELION, RADISH & FENNEL
196. SALMON SALAD
196. SUPER STAR GREENS
197. SEAWEED WRAP
197. TUNA OR MACKEREL SALAD
197. TURKEY WRAP

STARCH

GRAINS, RICE & QUINOA
198. KALE ON THE WILD SIDE
198. CURRY QUINOA SALAD

SANDWICHES & SNACKS
199. SPREADS FOR STARCH
199. BEANS
199. BREAD
199. RICE
199. VEGGIE

PROTEIN
200. DAIRY
200. EGGS
200. BACON
200. CHICKEN
200. FISH
200. MEAT
201. SALMON
201. TUNA
201. TURKEY
201. VEGGIES AND DIPS

Bread

Bran Bread

Combine and blend (I use a food processor)
- 1 cup whole wheat flour
- ¾ cup almond flour
- ¾ cup all bran cereal
- 2 tablespoons powdered milk
- 1 packet active dry yeast
- 1½ teaspoons salt

Stir together in separate bowl
- 1⅓ cup water (+ 1 teaspoon if needed)
- 1½ tablespoons molasses
- 2 tablespoons walnut, peanut or olive oil
- 1 *Canna Chinese Five Spice Blend*

Slowly blend into the flour mixture, let sit 1 hour

Place in a well-oiled covered bowl in warm area to rise for 1 hour. Punch down, sprinkle with almond flour and bake in a well-oiled loaf pan at 400°F for 30-45 minutes. Check for doneness: a thumb print should bounce back up. Cool on a rack.

Breakfast Blueberry Muffins

Combine
- 1½ cups whole wheat pastry flour
- 1 *Canna Spicy Jelly Spice Blend*
- 1 tablespoon baking powder
- 4 tablespoons stevia
- ¼ teaspoon salt

Add & mix
- 1 egg
- 1 cup milk
- 1 teaspoon vanilla
- 6 tablespoons honey
- 5 tablespoons *Canna* Coconut Oil (Ch.2, pg.32) softened
- 1 cup *Canna* Honey Walnuts, chopped (Ch.8, pg.211)

Fold in
- 1 cup blueberries

Line muffin tin with 12 baking cups, spray with oil and fill, bake at 400°F for 18-22 minutes.

Spice Carrot Bread

Heat on low for 10 minutes
- ¾ cup coconut oil
- 1 *Canna Spicy Jelly Spice Blend*

Whisk in then set aside to cool
- ⅔ cup stevia

Mix and beat until smooth
- 2 eggs
- ½ teaspoon salt
- ½ teaspoon ginger, minced
- 1 teaspoon vanilla
- ¾ teaspoon baking powder
- ½ teaspoon baking soda
- Cooled spiced oil

Stir in one at a time
- 2 cup whole wheat flour (add in small amounts)
- 1½ cup carrots, shredded
- ½ cup pineapple, chopped small
- 1 cup *Canna* Spicy Jelly Spiced Nuts (Ch.8, pgs. 206-211), chopped

Place into greased loaf pan and bake at 300°F for 1 hour or until toothpick comes out clean.

Lemon Butter Crumbs Vegan

Combine
- ½ cup whole wheat bread crumbs
- 1 *Canna Lemon Pepper Spice Blend*
- 3 tablespoons olive oil or butter
- 1 teaspoon lemon zest
- 2 tablespoons nutritional yeast flakes
- ¾ teaspoon salt

Spread out onto a sheet and bake at 350°F for 10 minutes or top your favorite recipe before baking.

Spicy Bran Crumbs

Follow the Lemon Butter recipe (Pg. 163) substituting *Canna Chili Spice Blend* in the place of the Lemon Pepper.

Zucchini Bread

In sauce pan heat to a soft boil
    2⅓ cups nonfat milk
    ⅓ cup heavy cream
Add to soft boiling milk, whisk and simmer on low for 10 minutes
    2 *Canna Fruit Pie Spice Blend*
    ¾ cup honey or stevia
    2 tablespoons vanilla extract
    ¼ cup molasses
Mix in, and then set aside
    2 cups rolled oats
In separate bowl, combine then add to milk mixture
    2 cups all bran cereal
    2 small zucchinis, shredded
Add to milk mixture and blend
    2 small carrots, shredded
    32 ounces nonfat yogurt, plain
In a separate bowl, mix then add to the milk mixture and blend well until a ball is formed
    4 cups whole wheat flour
    2½ teaspoons baking soda
    2½ teaspoons baking powder
    2 teaspoons orange
    1 tablespoon lemon zest
    3 tablespoon lemon juice
    2 cups *Canna* walnuts (Ch.8, pg.211)

Spray oil on all sides of a 8x11 baking pan, fill with the batter and bake at 400°F for 10 minutes, than continue baking another 20 minutes at 350°F. If you are looking for a little more symptom relief try adding additional cannabis to your next batch. When baking, exact measurements, altitude, humidity and oven temperature can alter the finished results.

Crepes & Pancakes

Crepes

Heat for 10 minutes on low, cool
        1 *Canna Fruit Pie Spice Blend*
        2 tablespoons coconut oil
Whisk in   2 large eggs
        2¼ cups skim milk
        ½ teaspoon vanilla
        ½ teaspoon vanilla
Combine, and set aside
        1½ cups whole wheat pastry flour
        3½ tablespoons stevia
        Pinch of salt

Blend flour and milk mixtures together and chill for 1 hour. On medium high in 2 tablespoons of coconut oil, cook each crepe 1 minute, flip and cook 30 seconds, layer on wax paper until all are cooked and fill with your favorite compote.
Finish with *Canna* Whipped Cream (pg. 283).

Rum Raisin Nut Pancakes

Heat and whisk on low for 10 minutes, set aside to cool
        2 tablespoons coconut oil
        1 *Canna Fruit Pie Spice Blend*
        ½ cup skim milk
Blend in   ½ cup whole wheat flour
        ¼ cup toasted bran
        ¼ cup rolled oats
        ½ teaspoon baking powder
        ¼ teaspoon salt
Beat   2 eggs
Add to   Flour and spice milk mixture
Mix in   1 cup *Canna* Raisin Rum Nuts, chopped (Ch.8, pg.206-211)

Lightly oil a flat skillet and fry dollar size cakes until golden on both sides. Serve with nonfat yogurt, cottage cheese or sugar free jam, maple syrup or honey. My favorite topping is nonfat yogurt with vanilla and stevia, topped with sugar-free Strawberry Jam (Ch.10, pgs. 272-275).

Pineapple Pancakes

Heat and whisk on medium high until butter browns, about 2 minutes
    2 tablespoons unsalted butter or Ghee
    1 *Canna Spicy Jelly Spice Blend*
    1 tablespoon stevia
    ½ teaspoon molasses

Brown 4-5 minutes each side, remove from heat
    1 pineapple cored and sliced ½ inch thick, reserve syrup

Add   ¾ cup *Canna Dark Rum* (Ch.6, pg.142)
    ¼ cup stevia

Return to medium high heat and cook until thick and bubbly. Transfer pineapple to a plate and reserve syrup.

Pancake; Heat oven to 325°F with rimmed pan and wire rack for warming

Combine   1 cup whole wheat pastry flour
    1 teaspoon baking powder
    1 teaspoon baking soda
    3 tablespoons stevia
    1 teaspoon salt

Whisk together
    1 large egg
    ½ teaspoon vanilla
    1 cup buttermilk or heavy cream

Combine flour and egg mixture. Cook on medium high with nonstick spray in batches until golden brown and bubbles form on top. Top each pancake with 1 pineapple ring before turning. Place in oven on rack and bake until done, about 5 minutes.

Serve with warm Syrup, mixed with reserved pineapple juice.

Pumpkin Pancakes

Combine   2 cups whole wheat pastry flour
    1 *Canna Spicy Jelly Spice Blend*
    1 tablespoon baking powder
    2 tablespoon stevia
    ¼ teaspoon salt

Whisk together
    2 large eggs
    1¾ cups skim milk
    ½ cup pumpkin, puree
    3 tablespoons coconut oil, softened

Combine and cook on a hot oiled griddle until brown.

NOTES

Crackers

Almond Crackers GF

Mix	1½ cups almond meal
	3 tablespoons *Canna* Fruit Pie Spice Butter (Ch.2, pg.30-31)
	2 teaspoons stevia
	2 tablespoons *Canna* Almonds, crushed (Ch.8, pg.206-211)

Press and pat into baking pan. Score into 2-inch squares and brush with additional *Canna* Spice Butter and bake at 350°F for 20 minutes. Cool and break into 2-inch pieces and store in airtight container.

Quick Bar-B-Que Crackers Vegan

Mix well with a fork in a baking pan	
	1 cup whole wheat flour
	¼ teaspoon salt
Add	⅓ cup olive oil
	1 *Canna Bar-B-Que Spice Blend*
	3 tablespoons ice water

While mixing the flour, slowly add the oil mixture and blend well in the pan.
Press into baking pan until smooth and even. Brush with *Canna* Bar-B-Que Spice Blend Oil (Ch.2, pg.32). Bake at 350°F for 15-20 minutes

Taco Chips Vegan

Combine	4 tablespoons olive oil
	1 *Canna Taco Spice Blend*
Coat	6 pitas cut into 2 inch pieces

Bake on a cookie sheet at 300°F for 15 minutes.

Sweet Cinnamon Crackers

Combine and blend in food processor
        2½ cups whole wheat pastry flour
        4 teaspoons stevia
        2 teaspoons salt
Blend   1 *Canna Spicy Jelly Spice Blend*
        ½ cup butter or ghee

Add butter spice to the processer with flour and blend adding ¼ cup sprinkles of ice water while blending. Split dough in two, cover and refrigerate for 1 hour or freeze for later. Roll dough between parchment paper ¼-inch thick, adding flour if needed for sticking. Brush with melted butter. Score into 2- inch squares, sprinkle with stevia and bake at 425°F for 15-20 minutes until slightly brown. Cool and break at score.

Quick Bran Crackers Vegan

Combine in a baking pan and mix
        ¾ cup whole wheat flour
        ¼ cup wheat bran
        ¼ teaspoon salt
Add to measuring cup
        3 tablespoons ice water.
        ⅓ cup *Canna* Italian olive oil (Ch.2, pg.32)

While mixing the flour, slowly add oil mixture and with a fork, blend well in pan. Press into baking pan, brush with *Canna* Olive Oil (Ch.2, pg.32). Prick with fork and score into 2-inch pieces, bake at 375°F for 20 minutes. Cool and break into squares.

Quick PB & J Graham Crackers

In baking pan mix
- ¾ cup graham cracker crumbs
- ¼ cup wheat bran.

Melt and whisk until dissolved
- 5 tablespoons *Canna* Spicy Jelly Butter (Ch.2, pg.30-31)
- 3 tablespoons stevia

Combine all together, mix well with a fork, press into pan, and score into 2- inch pieces and prick.
Bake at 375°F for 8 to 9 minutes.
Top with a smear of *Canna* Peanut Butter (Ch.2, pg.30-31) and Jam.

Flat Bread Crackers

Whisk
- 2 cups whole wheat pastry flour
- 1 *Canna Italian Spice Blend*
- 4 tablespoons stevia
- ¼ teaspoon salt

Cut in
- 6 tablespoons cold butter

Cut into small pieces with pastry blender or your fingers until it becomes coarse crumbs.

Add
- ¼ cup ice water
- 1 large egg yolk (save white for glazing the crust)

Add egg yolk mixture to the flour stirring with a fork until dough clumps; add traces of water if needed.

Knead 6 times on floured surface, make a ball, wrap in plastic wrap and chill for a minimum of 1 hour.
Line a baking sheet or pie pan with parchment or foil. Roll out dough and brush with butter and egg white, beaten

Sprinkle with   1 *Canna Italian Spice Blend*
Bake at 425°F for 20 minutes.

Rye Crackers

Combine   ½ cup whole wheat pastry flour
               2 teaspoons caraway seeds
               1 teaspoon baking powder
               ½ cup dark rye flour
               ½ teaspoon salt
Heat for 10 minutes, and then cool
               6 tablespoons butter
               1 tablespoon honey
               1 *Canna Savory Beef Spice Blend*
               3 tablespoons heavy cream

Work cooled butter into flour, little at a time until fully blended, do not over mix. Form into a ball and roll out between wax paper. Create shapes and place on ungreased cookie sheet 1 inch apart.
Heat for 15 minutes
               6 tablespoon butter
               1 *Canna Savory Beef Spice Blend*

Brush the dough shapes with *Canna* Butter (Ch.2, pg.31) and bake at 400°F for 5-6 minutes. Cool on rack and store in airtight container.

Oatmeal-Rolled Oats

Oatmeal GF

For added benefits, cook grains in *Canna* Tea (Ch.2, pg. 25-27).

Cook as directed on package.
- 2 cups dry oatmeal
- 3 teaspoons stevia
- 1 *Canna Fruit Pie Spice Blend*
- 2 tablespoons butter

Top with *Canna* Golden Gin Raisins (Ch.6, pg.143) and a dash of skim milk.

Honey Nut Granola GF-Vegan

Melt and whisk then remove from heat
- 2 tablespoons coconut oil
- 1 *Canna Spicy Jelly Spice Blend*
- ¼ cup honey
- 1 tablespoon stevia
- 1 tablespoon molasses
- ¼ apple, minced and smashed

Add
- 1 teaspoon vanilla
- 2 cup rolled oats
- ½ cup coconut, shredded
- ½ cup almonds, slivered
- ½ cup pecans, halved and chopped
- ½ cup walnuts, chopped
- ¼ cup pumpkin seeds
- ¼ cup sesame seeds
- ½ cup bananas, dried and chopped, (optional)

Pour wet mixture over oats and nuts, mix well. Pour onto parchment lined cookie sheet and smooth out (I use rubber gloves coated in coconut oil). Bake at 275°F for 45 minutes, stirring once. Break up and store in airtight container or freeze for longer storage.

Chocolate Chip Breakfast Cookie

Combine	1 cup rolled oats
	1 cup whole wheat flour
	1 teaspoon baking soda
	1 teaspoon salt
Blend in	½ cup *Canna* Jelly Spice Butter (Ch.2, pg.30-31), softened
	½ cup butter
In a separate bowl combine	
	¾ cup honey
	¾ cup molasses
	1 teaspoon vanilla extract
	2 beaten eggs
Fold in	2 cups dark chocolate chips
	2 cups *Canna* Spiced Walnuts (Ch.8, pg.206-211), chopped

Slowly add flour mixture to wet ingredients; mix well. Bake at 375°F for 10-12 minutes.

Dairy

Spiced Fruit Cottage Cheese GF

Warm on medium low for 15 minutes, then cool
  ¼ cup heavy cream
  1 *Canna Fruit Pie Spice Blend*
Drizzle over 2 cups cottage cheese, top with fruit

Peppered Cottage Cheese GF

Warm on medium low for 15 minutes
  ¼ cup heavy cream
  1 *Canna Lemon Pepper Spice Blend,* cool
Mix in ½ cup bell pepper, chopped
Drizzle over 2 cups cottage cheese
  Salt and pepper to taste, chill

Cheese Tortilla Chips GF

Heat on low for 10 minutes
  2 tablespoons ghee or unsalted butter
  1 *Canna Jamaican Jerk Spice Blend*
Toss in bowl ½ cup cheddar cheese, shredded
  ½ cup Parmesan cheese, shredded

Coat small omelet pan with ½ teaspoon of seasoned butter for each batch. Heat butter then sprinkle cheese evenly to cover base of pan, melt and brown 2 minutes, turn and brown.

Place on wax paper and score for chips or cool whole for a crispy tortilla.

NOTES

Eggs

If I was stranded on an island with my family and could have only one food source, it would be eggs.

Salmon Hash Bake GF

Prepare *Canna Lemon Pepper* Cauliflower Mash (pg. 232)
Prepare *Canna* Salmon, or use left overs

Combine   *Canna* Salmon, chunked
              1 onion, diced and sautéed
Spread out into a casserole pan, making 6 spoon indentations, and bake at 350°F for 10 minutes
Add   6 eggs into the spoon indentations
              ¾ teaspoon salt
              ¼ teaspoon pepper
Continue baking for another 10 minutes.
Serve over *Canna* sautéed greens (Ch.9, pg.235 or 241).

Boiled Eggs GF

Bring 6 eggs to a full boil. Cover, turn burner off and leave covered to steam for 10 minutes.
Drain and soak in ice water 10 minutes, crack and peel, being very careful to remove only the shell.

Curry Deviled Eggs GF

Boil, cool then cut in half, 8 eggs
Smash the yolks set aside
Simmer for 10 minutes
        3 tablespoons butter
        1 *Canna Curry Spice blend*
        3 tablespoons fresh squeezed orange juice

Add to egg yolks and blend until smooth, adjust thickness, fill egg cups and top with turmeric sprinkles.

Egg Salad GF

Boil   6 eggs, cool and chop
Sauté for 10 minutes then set aside to cool
            2 tablespoons unsalted butter or ghee
            1 *Canna Lemon Pepper Spice Blend*
Add all ingredients together, including:
            2 celery stalks, sliced
            2 green onions, sliced
            ½ cup mayonnaise
            ½ cup Greek yogurt
            2 tablespoons Dijon mustard
            Salt and pepper to taste

Dill Deviled Eggs GF

Boil, cool then cut in half 8 eggs
Smash the yolks and set aside

Simmer on low 10 minutes, let cool
            1 *Canna Pickling Spice Blend,* ground fine
            2 tablespoons butter
            3 tablespoons lemon juice
Add   2 tablespoons mayonnaise
            4 tablespoons celery, chopped fine
            1 teaspoon dill, chopped
            Smashed yolks

Fill egg cups and top with fresh dill for a nice presentation.

Sardine Deviled Eggs GF

Boil, cool then cut in half 8 eggs
Smash the yolks and set aside
Mix into smashed egg yolks
    3 tablespoons *Canna* Chinese Five Spice mayonnaise (Ch.5, pg.128)
    2 tablespoons *Canna* Chinese Five Spice vinegar (Ch.2, pg.32)
    3 tablespoons onions, minced
    4 sardines, smashed
    ¼ teaspoon pepper
    ¾ teaspoon salt
Fill egg cups and finish with
    ½ cup watercress

Crepes

Wheat-Free Crepes GF

Use this crepe in place of pancakes, tortillas and taco shells
Enjoy plain or roll up your favorite protein and veggie combination.

Simmer for 10 minutes
        3 tablespoons butter
        1 *Canna Spice Blend* (choose your favorite)
        3 tablespoons fresh lime juice
Add   8 eggs, beaten
        ¾ teaspoon salt
        ¼ teaspoon pepper
        Butter for pan

Pour onto a small omelet skillet over medium to medium high and cook until lightly browned 3 minutes. When lightly browned, very carefully turn egg pancake and cook another 1 minute. Continue until all eggs are gone, cover with foil and set aside.

Chinese Five Crepes GF

Fill *Canna* Chinese Five Spiced Crepes with grilled chicken, shrimp, bean sprouts, shredded red cabbage, green onions and watercress.

Curry Crepes GF

Fill *Canna* Curry Crepes with grilled shrimp, pineapple, bean sprouts, shredded red cabbage and watercress.

Italian Crepes GF

Fill *Canna* Italian Crepes with steak (sliced thin), shrimp, asparagus, olives, shredded red cabbage and watercress.

Taco Crepes GF

Fill *Canna* Taco Crepes with ground turkey, olives, cheese, black beans and cabbage.

Mushroom Crepes in Cheese Sauce GF

Sauté for 10 minutes, cover and set aside
    2 tablespoons unsalted butter or ghee
    1 *Canna Savory Beef Spice Blend*
    3 cups mushrooms, clean & trimmed and sliced
In sauce pan, bring to soft boil then remove from heat
    ½ cup heavy cream
Add   ½ cup fresh grated Parmesan cheese
    ½ cup goat cheese, grated
    ¾ teaspoon salt
    ¼ teaspoon pepper
Prepare *Canna* Crepes (pg.180-181). Divide mushroom mixture onto individual plates and top with *Canna* Cheese Sauce (Ch.5, pg.126).

Steak & Egg Crepes GF

Sprinkle   4 steaks with
    1 *Canna Savory Beef Spice Blend*
    ¾ teaspoon salt
    ¼ teaspoon pepper
Spray steaks on both sides with cooking spray and grill to medium, set aside to slice
Prepare   6 egg crepes (Ch.7, pg.180)
Heat over medium, set aside and keep warm
    2 cups lentils
Soft fry   1 tablespoon unsalted butter or ghee
    4 eggs
Layer; crepes, lentils and fried egg
    1 pepper jack cheese, sliced
    1 tablespoon salsa
    1 cilantro bunch, chopped
Top with sliced steak

Fried Eggs

Bacon, Spinach Fry GF

Sauté for 10 minutes, remove from heat and set aside
        8 ounces thick cut bacon, cubed
        1 *Canna Spicy Jelly Spice Blend*
        ½ cup onion, diced
        1 tablespoon stevia
Whisk into cooled bacon sauté
        2 tablespoons maple syrup
        3 tablespoons raw apple cider vinegar
Add and toss   4 cups spinach
Soft fry over medium heat
        1 tablespoon unsalted butter
        8 eggs
Serve 2 eggs on top of spinach
Top with   1 cup mushrooms, sliced and sautéed.

Poached Eggs
Fill a medium pot with 2 inches of water, bring to a boil. Break each egg into a small ramekin or use an egg poacher. When water is boiling add 2 tablespoons raw apple cider vinegar, turn off heat. Using tongs, tilt ramekins and slide eggs in the water. Cover 2-3 minutes and remove with a slotted spoon to a towel. For a beautiful finish, trim the egg whites.

Salmon and Cream Cheese GF

Poach 4 eggs

Whisk over medium heat, then set aside
  2 tablespoons butter
  1 *Canna Chinese Five Spice Blend*
  8 ounces cream cheese, softened & smashed
Divide and layer on each plate
  4 ounces smoked salmon
  2 English cucumbers, thinly sliced
  Cream cheese mixture from above
  1 red onion, thinly sliced
  1 teaspoon capers
Top with poached eggs
Finish with 1 cup watercress
  ½ lemon, sliced

Spinach and Tomatoes GF

Heat over medium in a nonstick skillet
  2 tablespoons olive oil
  1 *Canna Lemon Pepper Spice Blend*
  ¾ teaspoon salt
Add and continue cooking for 5 minutes, set aside on a foil covered plate
  2 cups cherry tomatoes, halved
Add to warm skillet for 1-2 minutes
  4 cups spinach
Poach 4 eggs
Layer spinach, tomatoes, poached egg and finish with
  1 cup watercress, divided
  Salt and pepper to taste

Quiche

Quick and Easy Lemon Pepper Crust Vegan

Combine and mix in pie pan
        1 cup whole wheat flour
        ¼ teaspoon salt
Mix well with fork using a separate bowl
        ⅓ cup *Canna* Lemon Pepper butter (Ch.2, pg.30-31)
        3 tablespoon ice water or *Canna* Tea (Ch.2, pg.25-27)

While slowly mixing the flour in the pie pan, add the butter mixture and blend well. Press into the pan until smooth and even. Prick with fork and bake at 375°F for 20 minutes; for pre-baked crusts, bake 10 minutes.

Quick and Easy Chili Bran Crust Vegan

Mix   ¾ cup whole wheat flour
        ¼ cup wheat bran
        ¼ teaspoon salt
Combine into a separate bowl
        5 tablespoons *Canna* Chili Olive Oil (Ch.2, pg.32)
        3 tablespoon ice water or *Canna* Tea (Ch.2, pg.25-27)

While mixing the flour slowly add oil mixture and blend well in the pan using a fork. Press into the pie pan, prick with fork and bake at 375°F for 20 minutes; for pre-baked crusts, bake 10 minutes.

Parmesan Kale Crust GF

Use for quiche, pies, wraps and so much more

Microwave for 30 seconds
- 2 tablespoons butter or ghee
- 1 *Canna Lemon Pepper Spice Blend*
- 1 tablespoon water

Whisk and add to butter and microwave additional 1 minute
- 2 eggs
- 4 to 6 kale leaves, chopped

Add ¾ cup Parmesan cheese, shredded

Press mixture into a pie pan and bake at 350°F for 10 minutes before filling or 20 minutes for a wrap.

Shrimp Broccoli & Leek Quiche GF

Prepare *Canna* Crust of your choice
Whisk over medium heat for 10 minutes
- 5 tablespoons unsalted butter or ghee
- 1 *Canna Chinese Five Spice Blend*
- ¾ teaspoon salt
- ¼ teaspoon pepper

Add and cook another 5 minutes
- 1 cup broccoli, small flowerets
- 1 leek, sliced

Add and cook 5 minutes
- 4 eggs, whisked
- ½ pound shrimp
- 1 cup jack or dill cheese, shredded

Pour soft egg mixture over kale or pie crust and press in with the back of a large spoon until all mixture is used. Bake at 350°F for 20-30 minutes. Cool and serve at room temperature.

Scrambled

Soft Scramble GF

Whisk   8 eggs
               1 *Canna Lemon Pepper Spice Blend*
               ½ cup heavy cream
               ¾ teaspoon salt
               ¼ teaspoon pepper

Heat in a nonstick skillet
               1 tablespoon unsalted butter
Add egg mixture, cook on low heat with gentle stirring until softly formed

Avocado Scramble GF

Whisk   8 eggs with
               1 *Canna Lemon Pepper Spice Blend*
               ¾ teaspoon salt
               ¼ teaspoon pepper

Heat a non-stick skillet
               2 tablespoons butter
Add egg mixture and cook until eggs are soft set
Top with   1 avocado, sliced
               1 hot pepper, minced (Ch.3, pg.73)
               1 cup watercress

Steamed

Tomato & Goat Cheese GF

Sauté over medium to medium high heat for 5 minutes
- 3 tablespoon olive oil
- *1 Canna Italian Spice Blend*
- ½ cup onions, minced
- ¼ teaspoon pepper
- ¾ teaspoon salt

Add and sauté another 5 minutes
- 1 red bell pepper, sliced thin

Add and simmer covered for 20 minutes
- 1 28 ounce tomatoes, Italian or plum, canned, drained

Reduce heat and simmer uncovered for 20 minutes or until slightly set. Stir, and then make 4 spoon indentations for the eggs.

Break
- 4 eggs into the spoon indentations
- ¾ teaspoons salt
- ¼ teaspoon pepper

Cover and cook until whites are set. Sprinkle with
- 1 cup goat cheese, crumbles

Finish with   1 cup watercress

Salads

Fruit and Vegetable Salads

Avocado Grapefruit GF-Vegan

Toss	1 cup cucumber, sliced
	2 tablespoons jalapeno peppers, minced
	¾ cup red onion, thinly sliced
	¼ teaspoon salt
Fold in	1 large grapefruit, segmented
	2 avocados, peeled and sliced
	2 tablespoons honey or stevia
	3 cups romaine lettuce
	3 cups watercress
Drizzle with	*Canna* Ginger Dressing (Ch.5, pg. 106)

Cucumber Salad GF-Vegan

Whisk	2 tablespoons *Canna* Lemon Olive Oil (Ch.2, pg.32)
	½ cup parsley, finely chopped
	3 tablespoons lemon juice
	¾ teaspoon salt
Toss with	1 cup cucumber, diced
	½ cup red onion, minced
	1 cup tomato, chopped

Jicama Sticks GF-Vegan

Try a squeeze of lime and chili powder. Bake or broil like a potato with *Canna Chili Spice Blend* and coconut oil for less starch, stir fry or enjoy raw.

Grape Balls GF

Freeze   3 cups grapes, red or purple

Heat 15 minutes, set aside to cool
         1 *Canna Spicy Jelly Spice Blend*
         3 tablespoons coconut oil
Cream   1- 8-ounce cream cheese, softened
Blend in   *Canna* Spiced Coconut Oil (Ch.2, pg.32)
Roll frozen grapes in cheese, freeze another 30 minutes on a cookie sheet.
Roll grape balls in
         2 cups *Canna* Nuts (Ch.8, pgs.206-211) chopped fine
Keep frozen until ready to serve.

Fruit Salad GF

Combine   ½ cup red grapes
         ½ cup red berries
         ½ cup mango
         ½ cup kiwi
         ½ cup orange
         ½ cup pineapple
Mix well, then toss with fruit
         ¼ cup Whipped Cream (Ch.10, pg. 283)
         ¼ teaspoon vanilla
         ¼ teaspoon stevia
         ¼ cup yogurt

Baked Kale Chips GF-Vegan

Toss   3 tablespoons *Canna* Spiced Oil (Ch.2, pg.32)
         1 tablespoon salt
         1 teaspoon pepper
         1 bunch kale, washed, dried & torn in bite size pieces
Bake on parchment covered cookie sheet at 350°F for 7-8 minutes.

Kimchi GF-Vegan

Add thinly sliced vegetables into a fermentation jar
- 2 Chinese cabbages
- 2 Chinese radishes
- 1-inch ginger
- 1 red hot pepper
- 2 onions

Mix well then add to slaw
- 2 *Canna Chili Spice Blend*
- ¼ cup stevia

Top with fermenting stone, cloth or vented fermenting lid and set aside for 3-6 weeks (until soft yet firm and to desired taste).

Kiwi Compote GF-Vegan

Pulse to coarse texture
- 5 kiwis, peeled

Simmer and stir over medium heat until thickened for 12-14 minutes; let cool.
- 2 tablespoons coconut oil
- 1 *Canna Fruit Pie Spice Blend*
- ½ cup *Canna* Golden Gin Raisins (next page)
- 3 tablespoons honey

Mix into kiwi, chill and serve over cottage cheese, fish or chicken.

Frozen Mango Slush GF-Vegan

Heat for 15 minutes, then cool
- 2 tablespoons coconut oil
- 1 *Canna Thai Spice Blend*
- 2 tablespoons stevia

Add, toss and freeze for two hours
- 3 mangos, smashed

Let defrost 10 minutes and blend to a slush.

Grilled Peach & Cheese Salad GF
Sounds crazy, but it's good!

Stir together and chill 30 minutes
    ½ cup mascarpone cheese
    2 tablespoons maple syrup, plus extra for drizzling
    1 teaspoon lemon juice
    ½ teaspoon lemon zest
    ¾ teaspoon salt
Prepare   4 large peaches, halved
Brush with   1 tablespoon coconut oil, softened
Sprinkle over peach halves
    1 *Canna Savory Beef Spice Blend*
Grill on low until dark brown grill marks.
Serve on a bed of greens with dollop of cheese, drizzle of syrup and finish with *Canna* Honey Walnuts (Ch.8, pg.211), chopped.

Gin Raisins GF-Vegan

Mix in a jar   1 cup gin
    1 *Canna Fruit Pie Spice Blend*
Add and shake 1 cup golden raisins
Refrigerate for up to 6 months
(See *Canna* Golden Gin or Rum Raisins, Ch.6, pg.143 and
Canna Raisin Rum Nut Sauce, Ch.10, pg.260)

Watermelon, Blueberry Salad GF-Vegan

In large bowl whisk and set aside for 15 minutes
    3 tablespoons *Canna* Lemon Olive Oil (Ch.2, pg.32)
    2 tablespoons *Canna* Apple Cider Vinegar (Ch.2, pg.32)
    1 tablespoon stevia
Add   2 cups watermelon, cubed
    1 cup peaches, sliced
    1 cup blueberries
    3 cups arugula
    3 cups watercress
    1 cup *Canna* Lemon Pepper Walnuts, chopped
    (Ch.8, pg.206-211)

Protein Salads

Bacon and Egg Salad GF

Combine and set aside
>1 cup spring mix salad greens
>1 cup watercress
>1 cup romaine

Sauté to crisp ½ pound bacon, cut into 1½ inch pieces
>1 *Canna French Spice Blend*
>½ cup onions, diced

Toss greens with bacon mixture and top with
>4 eggs, boiled and sliced

Curry Chicken Wrap GF

In fry pan combine
>3 chicken breasts, whole
>1 cup chicken broth
>1 *Canna Curry Spice Blend*
>¼ cup soy sauce, or amino acids
>1½ tablespoons Worcestershire sauce

Bring to a boil, cover, reduce heat and simmer for 15-20 minutes. Remove chicken from broth, drain and cool.

Drop into the hot chicken broth, immediately remove and lay flat on towel
>1 large bunch, spinach or kale

Shred cooled chicken and wrap in leaves, secure with tooth picks. Serve with *Canna* Curry Mayonnaise (Ch.5, pg.128).

Chicken Waldorf Salad GF

Rub   4 chicken breasts
                3 tablespoons olive oil
                1 *Canna Spicy Jelly Spice Blend*
Grill or bake for 25-35 minutes, let cool then cut into small pieces.

Slice and combine
                2 cups red grapes
                ½ cup *Canna* Golden Raisins (Ch.6, pg.143)
                ½ cup cheese, goat or blue
Whisk, then add
                ¼ cup *Canna* Italian Salad Dressing (Ch.5, pg.119)
                1 tablespoon stevia
Toss in   2 cups romaine lettuce, chopped
                2 cups iceberg lettuce, chopped
                2 cups dandelion greens
Add in chicken, serve

Coleslaw GF

Whisk together
                ½ cup *Canna* Lemon Pepper Mayonnaise (Ch.5, pg.128)
                ½ cup yogurt, plain
                ¾ teaspoon salt
                1 shake hot sauce
                3 teaspoons stevia
                ¼ teaspoon pepper
                1 tablespoon lemon juice
                2 tablespoons *Canna* Ginger Miso Dressing (Ch.5, pg.131)
Let meld in the refrigerator for at least 1 hour.

Add and toss   1 fennel bulb, thinly sliced
                4 cups cabbage, red or purple, shredded

Dandelion, Radish & Fennel GF

Whisk together
- 2 tablespoons *Canna* White Wine Dressing (Ch.5, pg.118)
- ¼ cup white wine, dry
- ¼ teaspoon pepper
- ¾ teaspoon salt

Chop and toss with dressing
- 2 bunches dandelion greens, young & tender
- 4 green onions, chopped
- 1 bunch radishes, sliced
- ½ fennel, thinly sliced

Salmon Salad GF

Combine together
- ½ cup onions, minced
- 1 stalk celery, diced
- 2 cans salmon, mushed
- ¾ cup *Canna* Greek Mayonnaise (Ch.5, pg.128)
- ¾ teaspoon salt
- ¼ teaspoon pepper

Chill 1 hour and serve wrapped in your favorite leafy greens.

Super Star Greens GF

Combine
- ¼ cup watercress
- ½ cup beets, sliced
- ½ cup avocado, diced
- 4 cups salad greens
- ¼ cup radishes, sliced
- ½ cup red onion, sliced
- ½ cup mushrooms, sliced
- ¼ cup *Canna* Seasoned Walnuts (Pgs .206-211), chopped
- ¼ cup *Canna* Lemon Pepper Olive Oil (Ch.2, pg.32)

Toss well and finish with crumbled goat cheese

Seaweed Wraps GF

Sauté for 10 minutes, remove from heat
        3 tablespoons sesame oil
        1 *Canna Chinese Five Spice Blend*
        2 inches ginger, peeled and shredded
Add & stir   ½ cup carrots, slivered
        1 hot pepper, minced, seeds removed
Add and stir   ½ cup brown rice, cooked
Wrap in nori rice mixture, including:
        ½ cup cucumbers, slivered
        2 cups watercress

Tuna or Mackerel Salad

        1 can tuna or mackerel, drained
        ¼-cup *Canna* Lemon Pepper Mayonnaise (Ch.5, pg.128)
        1 tablespoon hot pepper, minced (Ch.3, pg.73)
        Black pepper to taste

Turkey Wrap GF

Sauté for 10 minutes, set aside to cool
        3 tablespoons butter
        1 *Canna Savory Beef Spice Blend*
        1 hot pepper, minced, seeds removed
Add and mix   ¼ cup light mayonnaise
Layer over   8 romaine lettuce leaves
        Mayonnaise
        2 cups turkey, thinly sliced
        1 cup watercress
        2 tomatoes, thinly sliced
        Pepper to taste
Fold like a taco, adding another romaine leaf to each for stability and crunch.

Starch:
Grains, Rice & Quinoa

Kale on the Wild Side GF-Vegan

Cook 1 cup brown wild rice according to package directions.
Use chicken or vegetable broth in place of water, including;
    1 *Canna* Poultry Spice Blend
    2 tablespoons olive oil
Add to cooled rice
    ½ cup cranberries, dried
    1 cup kale, chopped small
    ½ cup *Canna* Spiced Walnuts (Ch.8, pg.211), chopped
Whisk and add into salad
    2 tablespoons *Canna* Flax Seed Oil (Ch.2, pg.32)
    2 teaspoons *Canna* Apple Cider Vinegar (Ch.2, pg.32)
    ¼ teaspoon pepper
    ¾ teaspoon salt
Serve at room temperature

Curry Quinoa Salad GF-Vegan

Cook quinoa according to the package directions. Use chicken or vegetable broth in place of water.
Sauté for 15 minutes
    2 tablespoons olive oil
    1 *Canna* Curry Spice Blend
    1 hot pepper, minced, seeds removed
Whisk in   4 tablespoons lemon juice
    8 tablespoons orange juice
    2½ tablespoons honey, warmed
    3 tablespoons red onion, minced
    ¾ cup *Canna* Gin Raisins (Ch.7, pg.193)
Make ahead and chill well
Toss in   ¾ cup *Canna* Curry Spiced Almonds (Ch.8, pg.208)

Sandwiches and Snacks

The real success with the sandwich is to stay true to food pairing
(See Ch.1, pg.13)

Canna Jamaican Mustard (Ch.5, pg.107)
Makes a great spread for sandwiches and starchy snacks.

Beans GF-Vegan (pair with rice and salsa)
- Wrap in soft greens
- Green and red bell peppers, chopped
- *Canna* Vegetarian Chili Burger (Ch.9, pg.226)

Hummus GF-Vegan
- Cucumbers, carrots, celery, radishes and jicama

Bread GF-Vegan
- Cheese, leafy greens and spread
- Tofu spread, red onions, thinly sliced
- *Canna* Dressing (Ch.5)

Tortillas GF-Vegan
- Black beans, cheese, salsa and parsley salad
- Brown rice, salsa, peppers and onions

French bread GF-Vegan
- Grilled with tomatoes, seasoning, fat-free cheese,
- Marinara sauce, olives and peppers

Rice GF-Vegan
- Brown rice and liquid amino
- Rice, skim milk, cinnamon and stevia, heated

Protein Snacks to Go

Wrap all protein in leafy greens or *Canna* Egg Crepes
(See Ch.7, pg.180)

Dairy GF
Chocolate milk with custard

Egg tortillas with cheese, apple or pear slices

Cheese and grapes

For cheese snacks, add a small smear of *Canna* Mayonnaise (Ch.5, pg.128) or *Canna* Mustard (Ch.5, pg.107)

Cheese finger wrapped in lettuce and watercress

Cheese wrapped with sliced turkey

Eggs GF
Boiled eggs, chopped with celery, onions & reduced calorie *Canna* Italian Dressing (Ch.5, pg.119)

Boiled eggs, bacon crumbles cheese, shredded lettuce *Canna* Mayonnaise (Ch.5, pg.128)

Canadian bacon GF
Canna Deviled Eggs (Ch.8, pg.178-179) and cheese *Canna* Mayonnaise (Ch.5, pg.128), onions, tomatoes and a little pineapple

Chicken GF
Canna Chicken Wings (Ch.9, pg.215)
Sliced chicken & kimchi

Fish GF
Onions, dill pickles and *Canna* Tartar Sauce (Ch.5, pg.133)
Canna Mackerel Salad (Ch.7, pg.196) and veggies

Meat GF
Any lean unprocessed meat, cheddar cheese & *Canna* Mustard (Ch.7, pg.107)

Salmon GF
>Salmon spread (Ch.5, pg.196)
>Red onions, capers and Cream Cheese

Tuna GF
Wrap in lettuce leaves
Canna Spiced Tuna (Ch.7, pg.196) green onions and celery

Turkey GF
Goat cheese, *Canna* Cranberry Chutney (Ch.10, pg.273) and sprouts

Swiss cheese, sauerkraut, *Canna* Mustard (Ch.5, pg.107) and sprouts

Veggies & Dips

Carrots, celery, cucumbers, endive, jicama and radishes for dipping; GF-Vegan

>Almond or Pumpkin *Canna* Butter (Ch.2, pg.30-31)

>Creamy Ranch Dressing (Ch.5, pg.132)

>French Lime Dressing (Ch.5, pg.128)

>Mix together *Canna* Caramelized Onions (Ch.9, pg.239), sour cream, cream cheese and green onions. Top with a dollop of *Canna* Sugar Free Jam (Ch.10, pg.272-275)

>Cranberries, *Canna* Goat Cheese (Ch.5, pg.127), sprouts

>*Canna* Peanut Butter (Ch.2, pg.30-31) and Sugar Free Jam

>Swiss cheese, Sauerkraut, or kimchi (Ch.7, pg.192) sprouts and *Canna* Mustard (Ch.5, pg.107)

Chapter 8: Nut about Nuts

SALT AND SAVORY
204. OREGON FRUIT & NUT MIX
204. ALMOND FRUIT PIE MIX
205. CHERRY CHOCOLATE MIX
205. CHILI PAW MIX
205. CURRY GINGER MIX
206. GINGER THAI MIX
206. ROASTED PEANUTS
206. PUMPKIN SEEDS

HONEY NUT & SEED MIXES
208. OREGON HONEY FRUIT & NUT MIX
208. HONEY BLUEBERRY OAT MIX
209. SPICY ALMOND CRANBERRY BARS
209. CHILI HONEY NUT MIX
210. PEANUT BUTTER & HONEY
210. SPICY PEANUT BUTTER CHOCOLATE CLUSTERS
211. HONEY PUMPKIN SEEDS
211. SPICY PISTACHIO & SEEDS
212. SPICY WALNUT GUAVA & MIX
212. SWEET HOT CHILI WALNUTS RAISIN

It's all about
Organic, Healthy, Sweet & Savory Snacks

We make such a big deal about nuts because they are a big deal! Always ready to eat, any time, any day. They are loaded to the max with vitamins and minerals and oh, so tasty!

With the many fruit & nut combinations available, here are some simple tips to help get you started:

- Mix well: spices, butter and oils along with sweeteners before adding nuts.
- 15 to 30 minutes is always an average baking time, but keep a close eye on the nuts for doneness.
- Always cool completely prior to storing.
- Unless otherwise stated, it is safe to store your baked goods in an airtight container at room temperature for one week, and refrigerate for up to 2 weeks.
- Combine our *Canna* Spice Blends to suite your personal taste.
- Nuts to Include: PAW (pecans, almonds, walnuts), peanuts and pistachio
- Seeds: chia, flax, pumpkin, sesame and sunflower
- Fruits: apples, blueberries, cherries, citrus zest, coconut, dates, cranberries, guava, pineapple, prunes and *Canna* Gin Raisins

Choose your favorite combinations & keep baking nuts!

Salty & Savory Nut Blends

Oregon Fruit & Nut Mix GF-Vegan

Heat for 5 minutes
- ½ teaspoon saffron
- 2 tablespoons olive oil
- 1 *Canna French Spice Blend*

Combine in a large bowl and toss with *Canna French* Oil
- ½ cup each: hazelnuts, almonds, pecans, walnuts and sunflower seeds
- 4 tablespoons candied ginger, shaved
- ½ cup blueberries, dried
- ½ cup cherries, dried

Spread on a lined cookie sheet and bake at 350°F for 20 minutes. Turn each 5 minutes, sprinkle with salt and toss.

Almond Fruit Pie Mix GF-Vegan

Place in plastic bag and shake to coat
- 2 tablespoons coconut oil, softened
- 2 cups mixed almonds, pecan and walnuts (PAW)
- 1 *Canna Fruit Pie Spice Blend*

Bake on a cookie sheet at 350°F for 15 minutes, turning once.
Mix together then add into the nuts
- 2 tablespoons apricots, dried and diced
- 2 tablespoons coconut, shredded
- ¼ cup cranberries, dried, chopped

Sprinkle with sea salt, toss and bake another 5 minutes.

Cherry Chocolate PAW Mix GF

Place in plastic bag and shake to coat
        1 ½ cups PAW
Mix   ½ cup sunflower seeds
        1 *Canna Spicy Jelly Spice Blend*
Add   2 tablespoons coconut oil, softened
        ½ cup cherries, dried and chopped
        ½ cup dark chocolate pieces
        2 tablespoons honey
Drop in bite-size mounds on a parchment lined baking sheet.
Sprinkle with sea salt and bake at 350°F for 15 minutes, turning once.

Chili PAW Mix GF-Vegan

Place in plastic bag and shake to coat
        2 cups PAW
        1 *Canna Chili Spice Blend*
Add   2 tablespoons coconut oil, softened
        5 tablespoons coconut, shredded
        ¼ cup dark chocolate pieces
        ¼ cup cranberries, dried, chopped
        2 tablespoons honey
Place in bite size pieces and bake at 350°F for 15 minutes, turning once.
Sprinkle with sea salt.

Curry Ginger Nut Mix GF-Vegan

Heat for 5 minutes
        2 tablespoons Coconut Oil
        1 *Canna Curry Spice Blend*
Add   2 tablespoons raw apple cider vinegar
Combine and shake well in a plastic bag
        2 cups mixed peanuts, pistachios and sunflower seeds
        ¼ cup candied ginger, diced
Place on a baking sheet, bake at 350°F for 20 minutes, turning once.

Ginger Thai Nut Mix GF-Vegan

Heat for 5 minutes
        2 tablespoons Coconut Oil
        1 *Canna Thai Spice Blend*
        ¼ teaspoon chili flakes
Add   2 tablespoons raw apple cider vinegar
Combine and shake well
        2 cups mixed peanuts, pistachios and pecans
        ¼ cup crystalized ginger, diced
Place on a baking sheet, bake at 350°F for 20 minutes, turning once.

Roasted Peanuts GF-Vegan

Place in plastic bag and shake to coat
        2 tablespoons coconut oil, softened
        1 *Canna Thai Spice Blend*
        2 cups peanuts
Bake at 350°F for 15 minutes, turning once.
Sprinkle with sea salt and toss.

Pumpkin Seeds GF

Place in plastic bag and shake to coat
        2 cups mixed pumpkin, sesame and sunflower seeds
        1 *Canna Spicy Jelly Spice Blend*
        2 tablespoons ginger, minced
        ½ teaspoon stevia
        ½ teaspoon coarse salt
        2 tablespoons butter or ghee, softened
Bake at 350° for 15 minutes, turning once.

Honey Nut & Seed Mixes

Oregon Honey Fruit & Nut Mix GF-Vegan

Heat for 5 minutes
    1 *Canna French Spice Blend*
    1 *Canna Spicy Jelly Spice Blend*
    ¼ cup coconut oil
    1/3 cup molasses
    1/3 cup honey
    1 teaspoon stevia
Combine in large bowl and stir with spices
    ½ cup each hazelnuts, almonds, pecans, walnuts & pumpkin seeds
    ½ cup cherries, dried, chopped
    ½ cup blueberries, dried
    ½ cup pears, dried, chopped
    4 tablespoons citrus zest
Bake on a parchment lined cookie sheet at 350°F for 20 minutes, turning each 5 minutes. Sprinkle with sea salt and toss.

Honey Blueberry Oat Mix GF-Vegan

In a large metal bowl combine then set aside
    1 pound PAW nuts
    1 cup blueberries, dried
    ¾ cup oats
Combine and heat for 10 minutes in a large, heavy skillet
    3 tablespoons ghee
    2 *Canna Fruit Pie Spice Blends*
    1½ teaspoons salt
    ¾ cup honey
    ½ cup stevia
Remove from heat, add to PAW nuts mixture and stir.
Separate into bite size chunks to cool

Spicy Almond Cranberry Oat Bars GF-Vegan

Heat for 5 minutes in a large heavy skillet until bubbly
> 4 tablespoons coconut oil
> 2 *Canna Chili Spice Blend*
> 1 tablespoon chili pepper flakes
> ⅓ cup honey
> 1 teaspoon salt

Add, stir with the honey mixture and remove from heat
> 2 tablespoons molasses, stir
> ½ pound almonds, roughly chopped
> ½ cup each sesame & pumpkin seeds
> ¼ cup each chia & flax seed meal
> ½ cup cranberries, dried
> ½ cup *Canna* Golden Gin Raisins (Ch.7, pg.193)
> 1 teaspoon vanilla

Press onto 2 parchment lined baking pans. Bake at 300°F for 30 minutes, remove from heat, cool. Place in the freezer for 15 minutes and cut into bars. Store in individual wrappers.

Chili Honey Nut Mix GF-Vegan

Place in plastic bag and shake to coat
> 2 cups mixed almonds, pecans & walnuts
> 1 *Canna Chili Spice Blend*

Place on a baking sheet, bake at 350°F for 15 minutes, turning once
Combine and toss with cooled nuts
> 2 tablespoons coconut oil, softened
> 5 tablespoons coconut, shredded
> ¼ cup dark chocolate pieces
> ¼ cup cranberries, dried and chopped
> 3 tablespoons honey
> Sprinkle with sea salt.

Peanut Butter & Honey GF-Vegan

Place in plastic bag and shake to coat
        2 cups peanuts
        1 *Canna Spicy Jelly Spice Blend*
Combine with 2 tablespoons peanut oil
        2 tablespoons honey
        ½ cup dried cherries, chopped
On a baking sheet, bake at 350°F for 15 minutes, turning once. Sprinkle with sea salt.

Spicy Peanut Butter Chocolate Clusters GF

Sauté over medium heat for 10 minutes
        3 tablespoons coconut oil
        1 *Canna Spicy Jelly Spice Blend*
        1½ cups peanuts
Add and heat 2-3 minutes
        2 tablespoons honey
Add   ½ cup peanut butter
Remove from heat and stir in
        ½ cup dark chocolate bites
Spread in a single layer on parchment paper and separate into small clusters. Cool and store in airtight container for up to 2 weeks

Honey Pumpkin Seeds GF-Vegan

Place in plastic bag, shake to coat
- 2 cups each pumpkin, sesame and sunflower seeds
- 1 *Canna Spicy Jelly Spice Blend*

Combine
- 2 tablespoons coconut oil, softened
- 2 tablespoons honey

Place on a baking sheet, bake at 350°F for 15 minutes, turning once. Sprinkle with sea salt.

Spicy Honey Pistachio Seed Mix my favorite

Combine in bowl
- ⅓ cup stevia
- 1½ teaspoons salt
- 1 *Canna Greek Spice Blend*

Heat in large heavy skillet
- ⅓ cup honey
- 2 tablespoons coconut oil

Add spice mix and remove from heat

Add
- 2 cups mixed PAW
- 1 cup pistachio nuts
- ¾ cup sunflower seeds

Press onto 2 parchment lined baking pans, separate nuts and pat flat. Bake at 300°F for 30 minutes, stirring every 5 minutes. Remove from oven, stir and separate.

Spicy Honey Walnut Guava Mix GF-Vegan

Combine in bowl
- ¼ cup stevia
- 1½ teaspoons salt
- 2 *Canna Jamaican Jerk Spice Blends*
- 1 tablespoon chili flakes
- 1 cup guava, dried, chopped

Heat on medium in large heavy skillet until bubbly
- ⅓ cup honey
- 2 tablespoons ghee

Combine stevia mix with honey and remove from heat
Add
- 1 pound walnuts
- ½ cup sesame seed

Press onto 2 parchment lined baking pans and separate nuts and pat flat. Bake at 300°F for 30 minutes, stirring every 5 minutes. Remove from oven, stir and separate. Store cooled nuts in airtight container.

Hot Chili Walnut Raisin Mix GF

Heat over medium heat for 15 minutes
- 2 tablespoons coconut oil
- 1 *Canna Spicy Jelly Spice Blend*
- 1 tablespoon chili pepper flakes
- 1½ cups walnuts
- ¼ cup sunflower seeds
- 1¼ cups raisins

Add and heat for 2-3 minutes while stirring
- 3 tablespoons honey

Remove from heat and add
- ¼ cup oats

Spread out in a single layer on a tray to cool and dry.
Store in an airtight container for up to 2 weeks.

Chapter 9: The Dinner Table

BACON
214. BACON, ONION & MUSHROOM

POULTRY
215. FRIED WINGS & GARLIC SAUCE
215. CHILI CHEESE BURGER WRAPS
215. QUICK TURKEY SAUSAGE
216. TURKEY LOAF & MUSHROOM
216. TURKEY DOG
216. TURKEY SHEPARD'S PIE
216. LOVE BUDS TURKEY SAUSAGE
217. TURKEY TACO WRAP

BEEF
218. FILET MINION & CAULIFLOWER
219. CHICKEN FRIED STEAK

WILD GAME
220. BUFFALO BLUE BACON BURGER
220. GINGERED VENISON WRAPS

LAMB
221. LAMB CHOPS

FISH & SEAFOOD
222. HALIBUT
222. FRIED OYSTERS
223. GREEK OYSTER BAKE
223. THAI OYSTERS
224. BAKED SALMON & DILL SAUCE
225. BAKED WHITE FISH & CHIPS

BEANS & LEGUMES
226. CHILI VEGGIE BURGER
226. BAR B QUE TEMPEH WRAP
227. CURRY VEGGIE BURGER
227. EDAMAME DILL STIR-FRY
228. SAVORY MUSHROOM TEMPEH
228. CHINESE TOFU CHOW MEIN
229. CURRY TOFU
229. TOFU TACOS

HOT VEGETABLES
230. BROCCOLI RABE
231. BOK CHOY STIR FRY
231. CABBAGE & ONION SAUTÉ
231. SWEET CARROTS
232. CAULIFLOWER MASH
232. FRIED CAULIFLOWER

233. CELERY ROOT MASH
233. EGGPLANT WITH MISO GINGER
233. FENNEL MASH

GREEN SUPER FOOD
234. BEET GREENS
234. DANDELION GREEN EGGS & HAM
234. GINGER BEANS
235. DANDELION ROOT & CELERY SAUTÉED
235. SAUTÉED KALE QUICK AND EASY
236. SWEET LEEKS

MIXED VEGETABLES
237. VEGGIE STIR FRY & WILD RICE
237. VEGGIE TACO
238. FRIED MUSHROOMS
238. MUSHROOM & GARLIC NOODLES
239. CRISPY SAGE ONIONS
239. CARAMELIZED ONIONS
239. WHIPPED PARSNIPS MASH
240. FRIED SAVORY ONIONS
240. RUTABAGAS
240. SAUERKRAUT & MUSHROOMS
241. SPINACH MUSHROOM SAUTÉ
241. PUMPKIN CURRY HAND PIES

SQUASH & SWEET POTATOES
244. SWEET ACORN SQUASH
244. TURNIPS & GREENS
245. SWEET POTATO STRINGS
246. SWEET POTATO FRIES & CHIPS

TOMATOES
250. ROASTED TOMATOES
250. TOMATO SAUCE

PASTA
251. BLACK BEAN PASTA
252. ITALIAN SPAGHETTI
253. SOBA NOODLE BOWL

RICE
255. CURRY WILD RICE
255. WILD RICE & VEGGIE STIR FRY

Bacon

Bacon, Onion & Mushroom Sauté GF

Sauté   ½ pound turkey bacon, cut into 1 inch pieces
1 *Canna Lemon Pepper Spice Blend*
3 tablespoons butter or ghee
1 onion, sliced
1 cup mushrooms, sliced

Serve over meat, poultry, fish, and beans, sautéed greens with eggs, or as a side.

Poultry

Fried Chicken Wings with Garlic Sauce GF

Prepare *Canna* Garlic Sauce (Ch.5, pg.105)

Shake   16 chicken wings, small end trimmed off
                   1 *Canna Curry Spice Blend*
Dip in   4 eggs, whisked
Roll in   *Canna* Curry Baking Coating (Ch.5, pg.124)
Fry on Medium high in 1 cup coconut oil, turning often.

Chili Cheese Burger Wraps GF

Brown in hot skillet
         1-pound ground turkey or beef
         1 *Canna Chili Spice Blend*
         1 hot pepper, minced
Add and bring to boil, simmer 10 minutes
         3 tablespoons water
Wrap browned meat
         8 large Romaine lettuce leaves double wrapped
         1 cup mozzarella or cottage cheese
         8 tablespoons *Canna* Tomato Sauce (Ch.9, pg.250)
         ½ red onion, thinly sliced

Quick Turkey Sausage GF

Simmer for 10 minutes
         1 *Canna Poultry Spice Blend*
         ¼ cup chicken broth
Add, brown   1 pound turkey, ground

Turkey Loaf with Mushroom Sauce GF

Mix   1 *Canna Savory Beef Spice Blend*
                 1 pound ground turkey
                 ½ teaspoon pepper
                 2 eggs, whisked
                 1 onion, diced
Pat into a loaf pan, bake at 350°F for 40 minutes
Prepare   *Canna* Mushroom Sauce (Ch.5, pg.125)

Turkey Dog no bun GF

Roll turkey sausage into hot dog shaped loafs and brown in coconut oil. Wrap in mustard, onions, sauerkraut, Swiss cheese and leafy greens

Turkey Shepard's Pie GF (Great dish for left overs)

Shape 4 *Canna* Love Buds Turkey Sausage patties (below)
Bake, grill or fry turkey patties, top with:
         Cauliflower Mash (Ch.9, pg.232)
         or *Canna* Acorn Squash Mash (Ch.9, pg.244)

Finish with   2 cups hot petite peas, divided

Love Buds Turkey Sausage GF

Mix   ½ pound beef, ground
                 ½ pound turkey, ground
                 ½ pound turkey sausage, ground
                 ¼ cup onions, dehydrated
                 ¼ cup celery, chopped small
                 ¼ cup peppers, dehydrated
                 1 tablespoon hot chili flakes
                 1 *Canna Savory Beef Spice Blend*

Form into patties and fry over medium-high for about 3 minutes on each side until well done. Wrap in greens and top with your favorite veggies or sauce.

Turkey Taco Wrap GF

Brown   2 tablespoons olive oil
           ½ cup onions, diced
Add and cook for 8 minutes
           1 pound *Canna* Turkey Sausage (Pg.216)
           or 1 pound turkey, ground
           1 *Canna Taco Spice Blend*
Add   ¼ cup green onions
           ½ teaspoon salt
           1 jalapeno or habanero pepper, minced
Wrap sausage mixture in
           8 romaine lettuces leafs
           1¼ cups American or Gouda cheese, shredded and split

Finish with   Salsa and Greek yogurt or sour cream

If you are not diabetic or in a weight loss program, you could substitute the lettuce with a wheat tortilla.

Beef

Filet Minion GF

Whisk and cook over medium heat for 10 minutes
>	4 tablespoons coconut oil
>	1 *Canna Savory Beef Spice Blend*

Rub steaks with spiced oil and set aside
>	4 steaks

Gravy
Whisk over medium heat for 10 minutes, set aside on warm
>	1 cup water
>	1 *Canna Savory Beef Spice Blend*
>	2 tablespoons xanthan gum

Grill Steaks, slice and blot with a paper towel to absorb excessive juices. Top steaks with *Canna* Cauliflower, *Canna* Gravy and greens.

Chicken Fried Steak & Gravy GF
Photo page 6

Coat	4-¼ pound steaks, pounded
	¼ teaspoon pepper
	¾ teaspoon salt
	3 eggs, beaten
Shake in	1 *Canna* Italian Baking Blend (Ch.5, pg.124)
Fry steaks in	4 tablespoons coconut oil until brown on each side.

Finish with *Canna* Mushroom Gravy (Ch.5, pg.125) adding ½ cup hot salsa.

Wild Game

Buffalo Blue Bacon Burger GF

Cook to crisp   ½ pound pepper bacon, and set aside
Add to drippings and sauté for 10 minutes
         1 *Canna Lemon Pepper Spice Blend*
In same pan cook to medium, set aside
         4 buffalo burgers
Add & sauté for 5 minutes
         1 cup red onions, sliced
         1 cup mushrooms, sliced
Layer on individual plates
         8 lettuce leafs, 2 per plate
         Burgers
         Mushrooms and onions
         1-2 tomatoes slices
Finish with bacon slices, watercress and blue cheese sprinkles.

Gingered Venison Lettuce Wraps GF

Brown	1 pound lean venison, ground
	1 *Canna Thai Spice Blend*
	2 tablespoons olive oil
Stir in	2 tablespoons liquid amino acids or soy sauce
	2 inch ginger root, peeled & grated
	2 green onions, chopped
	1 garlic clove, minced
	¼ cup hoisin sauce
	¼ teaspoon pepper
	¾ teaspoon salt

Serve this scrumptious gingered beef in crunchy lettuce wrap
Finish with   1 cup peanuts, chopped
                 1 cup watercress

Lamb

Lamb Chops GF

Mix   ½ cup olive oil
               1 *Canna Greek Island Spice Blend*
               2 tablespoons raw apple cider vinegar
Coat   8 thin or 4 thick lamb chops, set aside to rest for 1 hour
Grill or bake over medium high

Fish and Seafood

Halibut GF

Coat 4 halibut steaks
 1 *Canna Greek Island Spice Blend*
Sauté steaks 4 tablespoons butter for 3 minutes on each side, until white. Remove from pan and set aside
Add to pan, boil for 10 minutes
 1 cup heavy cream
 1 teaspoon dill
Add ½ cup white wine

Reduce to desired thickness and serve over greens.

Fried Oysters

Shake fresh, clean oysters
 1 *Canna Lemon Pepper Spice Blend*
 1 cup whole wheat flour
 ¼ cup toasted bran
 ½ teaspoon garlic
 ¾ teaspoon salt
Quick fry in hot peanut oil and butter mix until golden
 ½ cup peanut oil
 ½ cup ghee

Greek Oyster Bake GF

Mix   1 *Canna Greek Spice Blend*
               ½ cup softened butter or ghee
Roll oysters in the butter mixture
Shake in   *Canna* Baking Spice Blend (Ch.5, pg.124)
Bake, broil grill or fry until bubbly hot about 5-7 minutes

Thai Oysters

Stir together in a large bowl
           1 *Canna Thai Spice Blend*
           2 tablespoons peanut oil
           ½ cup roasted red peppers, julienned
           ½ cup peanuts
           1 pound oysters
Separate into oyster shells and bake at 350° for 5 minutes; broil on high another 5 minutes.

Baked Salmon & Dill Sauce GF

Coat   4 Salmon Steaks
               1 *Canna Greek Island Spice Blend*
Coat with cooking spray and bake 8 minutes at 350°F
Finish with   *Canna* Dill Sauce (Ch.5, pg.127)
                 Avocados, sliced

Oven-Baked White Fish and Chips GF

Whisk	4 eggs
	¾ teaspoon salt
	½ teaspoon pepper
Dip in egg	4 white fish filets
Roll in	1 *Canna* Italian Baking Spice Blend (Ch.5, pg.124)

Set aside on wax paper, fry in olive oil over medium 4 minutes, flip and cook 2 minutes
Serve over a bed of watercress greens

Beans & Legumes

Chili Veggie Burger GF; serves 6

Whisk over medium heat for 15 minutes, set aside
- ¼ cup butter or ghee, unsalted
- 1 *Canna Chili Spice Blend*
- 1 *Canna Bar B Que Spice Blend*
- 1 teaspoon salt
- ½ teaspoon pepper

In food processer, pulse
- ¼ cup parsley
- 1 carrot, chopped
- ¼ cup mayonnaise
- ½ onion, chopped
- 1 stalk celery, chopped
- 1 cup dandelion greens
- 1 green bell pepper, chopped
- 2-14-ounce kidney beans, canned
- 1 hot red pepper, minced (Ch.3, pg.73)
- Spice blend from above

Form into balls; smash into patties. Bake on parchment paper at 350°F for 25 minutes flipping halfway through. Alternatively, fry in sesame oil or grill on medium high.

Bar B Que Tempeh Wrap GF-Vegan

Sauté for 5 minutes
- 4 tablespoons coconut oil
- 1 *Canna Bar-B-Que Spice Blend*
- ½ cup celery, chopped

Add bring to a boil for 10 minutes
- 1-6 ounce tomato paste, canned
- 1-14 ounce tomatoes with juice, canned

Add   1 firm tempeh, cut into long shreds

Divide tofu mixture onto
- 4 kale leaves, softened

Finish with   watercress

Top with   *Canna* Fried Onions (Ch.9, pg.240)

Curry Veggie Burger GF, serves 6

Whisk over medium heat for 15 minutes, set aside
- ¼ cup olive oil
- 2 *Canna Curry Spice Blends*
- 1 teaspoon salt
- ½ teaspoon pepper

In food processer, pulse
- 2-14 ounce garbanzo beans, canned
- 1 red bell pepper, chopped
- 1 hot red pepper, minced
- 1 zucchini, chopped
- ¼ cup mayonnaise
- ¼ cup cilantro
- 1 celery stalk, chopped
- ½ red onion, chopped
- 1 cup kale
- Spice blend from above

Form into balls and smash into patties, sealing sides. Either bake on parchment paper at 350°F for 25 minutes, flipping halfway through, fry in sesame oil on medium high, or grill.
Serve with   *Canna* Yogurt Sauce (Ch.5, pg.131)

Edamame Dill Stir-Fry GF

Sauté on medium for 10 minutes
- 3 tablespoons sesame oil
- 1 *Canna Greek Island Spice Blend*
- ¾ teaspoon salt
- ¼ teaspoon pepper

Add, continue to sauté 5 minutes
- 1 celery, sliced
- ½ cup onion, diced

Add, bring to boil over low until desired consistency
- ¾ cup heavy cream
- 1 cup edamame, shelled

Reduce to a sauce. Serve with kimchi and *Canna* Fried Onions (Ch.9, pg.240)
Finish with watercress, green onions & dill sprigs

Savory Mushroom Tempeh GF

Sauté on medium for 10 minutes
- 4 tablespoons olive oil
- 1 *Canna Savory Beef Spice Blend*
- ½ teaspoon pepper
- ½ teaspoon salt
- 1 onion, diced
- 2 cups mushrooms, sliced

Add, bring to a boil, and simmer until desired thickness
- 1 package tempeh, firm, cut into 1 inch cubes
- ¾ cup heavy cream

Serve over greens & steamed carrots
Finish with   *Canna* Fried Mushrooms (Ch.9, pg.238)
Canna Fried Onions (Ch.9, pg.240)

Chinese Tofu Chow Mein GF-Vegan

Sauté for 10 minutes
- 4 tablespoons peanut oil
- 1 *Canna Chinese Five Spice Blend*
- 1 fennel bulb, thinly sliced and diced
- 1 green pepper, diced
- 1 cup celery, chopped
- 1 onion, diced

Add, bring to a boil
- 1 cup chicken broth

Whisk in   ¼ cup xanthan gum
Serve over brown rice
Top with   1 cup bean sprouts
½ cup green onions, diced

Curry Tofu GF-Vegan

Sauté for 5 minutes
    3 tablespoons peanut oil
    1 *Canna Curry Spice Blend*
    1 cup sweet potatoes, cubed
    1 cup celery, diced
    1 cup tofu, cubed
    ¼ teaspoon pepper
    ¾ teaspoon salt

Add, bring to a boil, cover and simmer on low 40 minutes
    ½ cup brown rice
    1 ½ cups chicken or vegetable broth
Remove the lid, simmer until desired thickness.
Serve over   dandelion greens
Finish with   *Canna* Fried Sweet Potatoes Strings (Ch.9, pg.245)

Tofu Tacos GF-Vegan

Sauté   4 tablespoons coconut oil
    1 *Canna Taco Spice Blend*
    1 hot pepper, minced (Ch.3, pg.73)
    1 red bell pepper, chopped
    ½ cup celery, chopped
Bring to a low boil for 10 minutes
    1-6-ounce tomato paste, canned
    1-14 ounce tomatoes with juice, canned
Add, stir   1 box tofu, firm, cut into long shreds
Divide tofu mixture onto
    4 soft kale leaves or *Canna* Crepe Tortillas (Ch.7, pg.165)
Top with   shredded lettuce & jack cheese

Hot Vegetables

Broccoli Rabe GF-Vegan

Sauté blanched broccoli in olive oil with your choice of any *Canna Spice Blend* for 10 minutes. Serve alone or as a side. Add to soup or pasta, dried figs and toasted pine nuts. Sprinkle ricotta cheese, other dried salted cheese or goat cheese and pepper to taste. Enjoy the softer flavor and is a bit easier to digest than its twin, broccoli.

Bok Choy Stir Fry GF-Vegan

Sauté for 5 minutes
        4 tablespoons sesame oil
        1 *Canna Chinese Five Spice Blend*
Add   1 cup leeks, whites only, sliced
        1 cup celery, diced
        2 tomatoes, diced
        1 head bok choy, chopped into 1½ inch pieces
Sauté for 8 minutes. Use amino acids in place of soy sauce. Great with tofu, poultry or seafood.

Cabbage & Onion Sauté GF-Vegan

Sauté   4 tablespoons butter or olive oil
        1 *Canna Lemon Pepper Spice Blend*
Add   2 onions, sliced
Sauté until brown
Stir in   1 head cabbage, thinly sliced
Cover and simmer for 20 minutes

Sweet Carrot Sauté GF-Vegan

Sauté   1 *Canna Savory Beef Spice Blend*
        ¼ cup butter or olive oil
Add, sauté until brown and stir stir
        2 cups carrots, sliced
Sprinkle with   1 tablespoon stevia
Cook 15 minutes on low until carrots remain semi-firm

Cauliflower Mash GF potato substitute

Boil, until nearly soft. Strain and set aside
    1 cauliflower, cut up into 2 inch pieces
Cook 15 minutes on medium
    ⅓ cup butter or ghee
    1 *Canna Lemon Pepper Spice Blend*
Mash fully drained cauliflower into butter mixture with
    Lemon zest
    ¾ teaspoon salt
    ¼ teaspoon pepper

My favorite addition to cauliflower mash:
Add   2 tablespoons grated horseradish (adds the Wow!)

Fried Cauliflower GF

Fry until 4 slices are brown on both sides, set aside
    3 tablespoons hot butter
    1 large head cauliflower, sliced ½ inch thick

Boil remaining cauliflower for 10 minutes
    1 cup chicken broth
    Cauliflower flowerets
    1 *Canna Spicy Jelly Spice Blend*
Add & puree   1 teaspoon salt
    ½ teaspoon pepper
Add back   fried cauliflower slices to boiling broth
Cover and simmer 15 minutes
Add   1 cup heavy cream

Bring back to soft boil and simmer until reduced to a creamy consistency

Celery Root Mash GF Serve in place of potatoes

Boil for 15 minutes, drain thoroughly and set aside
        4 celery roots, quartered
Cook for 15 minutes on medium low
        ⅓ cup butter
        1 *Canna Lemon Pepper Spice Blend*
        ¼ teaspoon pepper
        ¾ teaspoon salt

Add celery root to butter and mash
Add   ¼ cup mayonnaise for creamy texture

Eggplant with Miso Ginger Sauce GF-Vegan

Fry until brown
        2 eggplants, sliced
        Canna Butter, Ghee or olive oil (Ch.2, pg.31-32)
Top with   *Canna* Ginger Miso Yogurt Sauce (Ch.5, pg.131)

Fennel Mash GF-Vegan

Cook on medium for 10 minutes and set aside
        2 fennel bulbs, cubed with greens removed
        1 cup chicken broth

Melt   ¼ cup butter or olive oil
        1 *Canna Chinese Five Spice Blend*
Add   ¼ cup mayonnaise and whisk

Strain fennel and mash until very small chunks. Stir in butter mixture. Salt to taste

Green Super Food

Beet Greens GF-Vegan

Sauté   4 tablespoons olive oil
                1 *Canna Lemon Pepper Spice Blend*
                4 cups smaller tender green leaves, chopped
Add   ½ cup *Canna* Golden Raisins (Ch.7, pg.193)
                ½ cup *Canna* Honey Walnuts (Ch.8, pg.211)

Dandelion Green Eggs & Ham GF

Boil 4 eggs (Ch.7, pg.177)
Sauté for 10 minutes
         4 tablespoons olive oil
         1 *Canna Chili Spice Blend*
         1 onion, chopped
         ½ pound turkey ham, cut into thick ribbons
Add and sauté until tender
         1 bunch dandelion greens, cleaned and trimmed
         Salt to taste
Top each serving with a sliced boiled egg & sprinkle of cayenne.

Ginger Beans GF-Vegan

Sauté over medium high heat for 3 minutes
         1 *Canna Lemon Pepper Spice Blend*
         1 tablespoon ginger, minced
         3 tablespoons sesame oil
Add   1 pound fresh green beans

Continue to sauté for 5 minutes. Serve with chicken, fish or beef.

Dandelion Root & Celery Puree GF

Steam for 20 minutes
        1 dandelion root, chopped
        2 cups celery, chopped
Remove from steamer, drain and mash until chunky smooth
In a separate pan, heat on medium for 10 minutes
        1 *Canna Thai Spice Blend*
        ¾ teaspoon salt
        ¼ teaspoon pepper
Add   ¾ cup butter or ghee
        ¼ cup heavy cream

Combine with dandelion root and celery. Serve under a steak, salmon or tuna.

Quick & Easy Sautéed Kale GF-Vegan

Sauté until wilted
        4 tablespoons olive oil
        1 *Canna Lemon Pepper Spice Blend*
        1 bunch kale, large, torn into 2 inch pieces
Remove from heat
Add, then serve
        2 tablespoons raw apple cider vinegar

Sweet Leeks GF-Vegan

Sauté	1 *Canna Fruit Pie Spice Blend*
	1 teaspoon chili flakes
	2 tablespoons olive oil
	1 tablespoon stevia
Add	4 cups leeks, cut into 1" pieces
Add, cook for 10 minutes	
	½ cup chicken broth, fat free

Mixed Vegetables

Veggie Stir Fry & Curry Wild Rice GF-Vegan

Cook over medium heat for 10 minutes
      ½ cup vegetable or chicken broth
      1 *Canna Curry Spice Blend*
      1 tablespoon olive oil
Add   ¼ cup hot pepper, diced
      ½ cup yellow squash, cubed
      ½ cup asparagus, cut into 1 inch pieces
      ½ cup broccoli, par boiled florets
      ½ cup eggplant, cubed

Sauté until vegetables are tender crisp
Prepare *Canna* Curry Wild Rice (pg. 255); top with mixed vegetables.

Veggie Tacos Vegan

Slice and sauté in olive oil
      2 poblano peppers
      2 yellow squash, chopped small
      1 white onion, diced
      1 hot pepper, minced, seeds removed
      1 *Canna Taco Spice Blend*
Add, stirring for 3 minutes
      1 cup mushrooms, sliced
      1 cup spinach

Heat whole wheat tortillas in skillet or grill with cooking spray.
Fill tortillas with veggies. Finish with tomato salsa, shredded jack cheese and squeezed lime.

Fried Mushrooms GF-Vegan

Combine & toss
        3 cups mushrooms, thinly sliced
        1 *Canna Savory Beef Spice Blend*
Fry in small batches on medium high in 1 inch of peanut oil. Fry 1-2 minutes, stir, and keep separated. Remove to paper towel, and keep separated. Perfect condiment for topping salad, fish, meat & legumes.

Mushroom & Garlic Noodles

To make this a perfectly paired meal, replace the oil with vegetable broth.

Whisk and sauté on medium for 2 minutes
        2 tablespoons olive oil or broth
        1 *Canna Italian Spice Blend*
Add   3 cups milk, nonfat
Whisk in   3 tablespoons flour, whole wheat
Add, bring to a soft boil. Cook and stir over medium low until sauce thickens, about 30 minutes.
        5 cloves garlic, minced
Add cover and set aside
        1 pound mushrooms, sliced
        1 can tomatoes, diced
        1 cup ricotta cheese chunked
        ¼ teaspoon pepper
        ¾ teaspoon salt
Boil   1 handful noodles, whole wheat
        4 cups *Canna* Tea (Ch.2, pgs.25-27)
Cook until al dente. Do not overcook. Strain
Toss in   2 tablespoons olive oil or broth

Add in mushroom mix and serve over sautéed greens.
Finish with ¼ cup feta or goat cheese

Crispy Sage Onions GF-Vegan

Shake   4 large onions, thinly sliced
               1 *Canna Poultry Spice Blend*
               2 tablespoons coconut oil at room temperature
Heat in large pot over medium high
               1 cup coconut oil

Add half of the onions, a little at a time to keep onions from sticking. Stir to keep loose. When crispy dark golden brown, remove to a paper towel and add the second batch.

Caramelized Onions GF-Vegan

In large nonstick skillet, sauté on low 2 hours
               2 tablespoons olive oil
               1 *Canna Chili Spice Blend*
               6 onions, large, sliced
               ¼ teaspoon pepper
               ¾ teaspoon salt

Whipped Parsnip Mash GF-Vegan
Replaces white potatoes

Boil until tender firm, drain
               4 parsnips, cut into large cubes
Add   1 *Canna Lemon Pepper Spice Blend*
               ¼ cup butter, ghee or coconut oil

Mash, cover and set aside.
Optional: add shredded carrots, ginger, chopped spinach or other greens.

Fried Savory Onions GF-Vegan

Combine   2 onions, large thinly sliced
                1 *Canna Savory Beef Spice Blend*

Fry in small batches in 1 inch of peanut oil until crispy golden brown.
Remove to paper towel, keep separated.
Perfect condiment for topping salad, fish, meat and legumes.

Rutabagas GF-Vegan

Boil till tender 4 rutabagas, cubed

Toss with   ½ cup *Canna* Honey Walnuts (Ch.8, pg.211)
                ¼ cup *Canna* Gin or Rum Raisins (Ch.6, pg.143)

Sauerkraut Mushrooms & Onions GF-Vegan

Sauté for 15 minutes on medium-low heat
                6 tablespoons olive oil
                1 *Canna Savory Beef Spice Blend*
Add   3 onions, sliced
                2 cups mushrooms, sliced
Sauté another 15 minutes
Add   2 cups sauerkraut, stir
Serve over sautéed greens for a veggie meal or as a side to grilled meat

Spinach Mushroom Sauté GF

In a medium fry pan, sauté on medium heat for 15 minutes
- 3 tablespoons butter
- 1 *Canna Lemon Pepper Spice Blend*

Add   1 cup sliced mushrooms
While whisking, add
- 1 tablespoon molasses
- 1 tablespoon stevia
- 1 tablespoon red wine vinegar

Add   1 handful spinach (total 2 bunches)
Add   handful spinach

Pumpkin Curry Hand Pies

Prepare *Canna* pie crust (pgs. 185-186) enough for 3 single crusts

Bake at 375°F for 30 minutes on an oiled rimmed pan
- 6 cups pumpkin, cubed

Cook over medium heat
- 5 tablespoons coconut or olive oil
- 1 *Canna Curry Spice Blend*
- 1 large onion, chopped

Add pumpkin to spice mix, cook 5 more minutes
Add   ½ cup *Canna* Golden Rum Raisins (Ch.6, pg.143)

Mash pumpkin together with a spoon and set aside
Roll out 3 pie crusts to 10 inches, cut each in half. Divide pumpkin mash onto 6 pie sections and seal all sides. Line 2 baking sheets with parchment paper and bake 3 to a sheet at 375°F for 15-20 minutes. Serves well with a crisp salad.

NOTES

Squash & Potatoes

Sweet Acorn Squash GF

Dissolve   2 tablespoons stevia
           2 tablespoons chicken broth
Add & whisk over medium heat
           ½ cup butter or ghee
           1 *Canna Fruit Pie Spice Blend*
           ¼ teaspoon pepper
           ¾ teaspoon salt
Add and whisk 2 tablespoons black strap molasses
Cut   2 squash in half, lengthwise, cleaned

Carefully fill squash ¾ full of butter mixture until 4 halves are filled, using a foil boat to level, if necessary. Bake at 350°F 1 hour.
Cool for 15 minutes. Mash the seasoning together with the squash and serve in the shell

Turnips & Greens GF-Vegan
Steamed, broiled, mashed or baked

Boil until tender
           4 turnips or rutabagas, cubed
Sauté   1 bunch turnip greens
           2 tablespoons butter or olive oil
           1 *Canna Curry Spice Blend*
Toss with ½ cup *Canna* Honey Walnuts (Ch.8, pg.211), chopped
           ¼ cup *Canna* Gin or Rum Raisins (Ch.6, pg.143)

Sweet Potato Strings GF-Vegan

Combine & toss

    2 sweet potatoes, peeled, thinly sliced
    1 *Canna Savory Beef Spice Blend*

Fry in small batches in 1 inch of peanut oil; keep separated. Remove to paper towel, keeping separate. This is a perfect condiment for topping salad, fish, meat and legumes.

Sweet Potato Fries & Chips GF-vegan

Cut   4 sweet potatoes, cut into long narrow strips or chip pieces, leaving skin intact.

Add & shake in a bag

         3 tablespoons *Canna* Olive Oil (Ch. 2, pgs. 33-34)
         1 *Canna Bar-B-Que Spice Blend*

Spread out on baking sheet. Bake at 400°F for 15 minutes and flip. Lower heat to 350°F and continue baking another 10 minutes until crisp.

NOTES

Tomatoes

Roasted Tomatoes GF-Vegan

Slice 12 tomatoes in half and place on a baking sheet with sides. Top with olive oil, sprinkle with 1 *Canna Italian Spice Blend*. Bake at 250°F for 4 hours. Use in soup, sauce, a topping or side dish.

Tomato Sauce GF-Vegan
Great on anything: eggs, rice, pasta and zucchini noodles

Sauté	4 tablespoons olive oil
	1 *Canna Italian Spice Blend*
	¼ teaspoon pepper
	1 onion, chopped
	¾ teaspoon salt
Add	4 cloves garlic (after onions are soft and browned)
	4 fresh Roma or Italian style tomatoes or
	1-28 ounce Italian tomatoes, canned with juice
	1 cup tomato sauce

Bring to a boil, simmer 1-4 hours depending on your taste or desired thickness. Adjust the flavor with tomato juice, salt and pepper.

Pasta

I love pasta with everything, but when I combine pasta with meatballs, sausage, meat sauce or Alfredo sauce, it turns to sugar and sludge. Sludge in our systems causes bloat, pain, discomfort, gas, an irritable bowel, weight gain, and so many other problems you hardly know what's what! There are those who are on such a healthy whole food diet that the combination of poor food pairing does not seem to affect them; but for most of us foodies, this is not the case so we must follow some basic rules. Eat starch with vegetables and no fats. Eat protein with fats and vegetables.

To prepare pasta for optimum digestion and nutritional benefits, always leave it slightly under-cooked to al dente, never completely done. This brings a lower glycemic load than fully cooked pasta. Cook pasta in tea for an extra antioxidant boost.

Black Bean Pasta

Boil   1 pound whole wheat penne pasta
Halfway through, add and continue to boil for 3 minutes longer
                2 cups asparagus, cut into 1 inch pieces
Cook until pasta is al-dente, drain
Add   2 cups peas, frozen

Toss pasta & vegetables with *Canna* Black Bean Jerk Salsa (Ch.5, pg.115)
Top with a dollop of fat free ricotta cheese, cilantro and salt if needed.

Italian Spaghetti

Prepare *Canna* Italian Spaghetti sauce (Ch.5, pg.117)
Boil 1 pound whole wheat spaghetti noodles

Top the noodles with sauce and finish with fat free goat cheese and olives.

Soba Noodle Bowl GF-Vegan-Super Foods

Cook 8 ounces soba noodles as directed on package

Stir-fry over med-high for 5 minutes
- 2 tablespoons peanut oil
- 1 *Canna Chili Spice Blend*
- 12 brussel sprouts, trimmed & halved
- 1½ tablespoons water

Add & stir fry for 3 minutes
- ½ cups mushrooms, trimmed & halved
- 2 cups kale, trimmed and chopped
- 1 zucchini, small, halved and sliced
- 1½ tablespoons water

Stir in and continue cooking another 3 minutes
- ⅓ cup liquid amino acids or soy sauce
- 2 teaspoons ginger, minced

Remove from heat then add
- 1 tablespoon raw apple cider vinegar

Toss in the noodles

Finish with
- 2 teaspoon sesame seeds
- 1 red chili pepper, thinly sliced seeds removed

Rice

Curry Wild Rice GF-Vegan

Cook wild brown rice as directed on package

Sauté in order
    2 tablespoons coconut oil
    1 *Canna Curry Spice Blend*
    1 carrot, thinly sliced
    ¼ teaspoon pepper
    ¾ teaspoon salt
    ½ onion, diced
Add and bring to a boil
    1 cup coconut milk
Add   1 cup green beans, blanched
    ½ cup water chestnuts, or 1 can, sliced
Serve over rice, finished with
    ½ cup *Canna* Almonds (Ch.8, pg.206-211), sliced

Wild Rice and Veggie Stir Fry GF-Vegan

Cook wild brown rice as directed on package
Combine with the cooked rice and set aside
    ¾ cup cilantro, diced

Sauté in chicken broth for 5 minutes, in order
    1 *Chinese Five Spice Blend*
    ½ cup onion, diced
    1 cup broccoli, flowerets
Add in order until heated
    ¾ cup snow peas
    1 red pepper, sliced
    1 cup mushrooms, quartered
Serve over rice and finish with
    1 cup bean sprouts

NOTES

Chapter 10: Desserts

SPECIALTIES
259. BLUEBERRY MUFFINS
260. BANANA SPLIT
260. NUTTY AVOCADO
260. QUINOA BLUEBERRY NUT BAR
261. KIWI TART
261. LEMON HONEY & MANGOS
261. RAISIN RUM NUT SAUCE
262. GINGER BREAD COOKIES
263. GRAHAM NUT DESERT TOPPING
263. ZUCCHINI WALNUT LOAF

CHERRIES & CHOCOLATE
266. FROZEN DARK CHERRIES
266. CHOCOLATE FONDUE
266. CHOCOLATE NUT BAR
267. CHOCOLATE PEANUT DROPS
267. CHOCOLATE SAUCE
268. COCONUT ALMOND BARS
268. STUFFED SWEET DATES

FROSTING & FILLINGS
269. BITTER SWEET CREAM FILLING
269. BUTTER CREAM FROSTING
270. SWEET CREAM CHEESE FILLING
270. QUICK LEMON CREAM FILLING
270. FRUIT & CREAM DIPS
271. MAPLE MASCARPONE
271. SPICY WHIPPED FROSTING
271. QUICK VANILLA CREAM FILLING

OREGON FREEZER JAMS
273. CHERRY CRANBERRY CHUTNEY
273. OREGON STRAWBERRY JAM
274. RASPBERRY MINT JAM
274. OREGON STRAWBERRY TOPPING
275. BLUEBERRY JAM

PIE CRUST
278. ALMOND CRUST GF
278. QUICK BRAN PIE CRUST-VEGAN
278. QUICK PIE CRUST-VEGAN
279. FIBER PIE CRUST
279. QUICK GRAHAM-BRAN PIE CRUST
279. PUMPKIN PIE

POPSICLES
280. BANANA POPS
280. COCONUT POPS
280. PINEAPPLE POPS

YOGURT PARFAITS
282. FLAVORED YOGURT
282. LEMON FRUIT PIE
282. TOPPINGS
283. STRAWBERRIES & CREAM
283. WATERMELON & BERRIES

WHIPPED CREAM
284. WHIPPED CREAM
284. SPICED CREAM FROSTING
284. SPICED CRANBERRY CREAM

See these recipes for the best in dessert toppings:

Nuts	pg. 206-211
Rum Raisins	pg. 261
Jam	pg. 273-276
Cream, milk	pg. 138-139
Whipped cream	pg. 283
Pie crusts	pg. 278-279
Butter & oils	pg. 30-31

Specialties

Blueberry Muffins

Combine and Mix
- ¼ cup flax seeds, ground
- 1¾ cup flour, whole wheat
- ½ teaspoon baking soda
- ¼ teaspoon salt
- ¼ cup stevia
- 1 *Canna Spicy Jelly Spice Blend*

Whisk until smooth
- 2 large eggs
- ½ cup maple syrup

Add and whisk
- 1 cup yogurt, fat free
- ¼ cup milk, fat free
- ¼ cup coconut oil, softened
- 2 teaspoon orange zest
- 1 tablespoon orange juice
- 1 teaspoon vanilla

Add and blend flour mixture until just blended

Fold in
- 1½ cups blueberries
- 1 cup chopped *Canna* Honey Nuts (Ch.8, pg.211)

Spray and fill a 12 tin muffin pan, sprinkle with stevia. Bake at 400°F for 18-22 minutes until soft golden brown. Turn out on a wire rack to cool

Banana Split GF-Vegan

Choose colorful fruits for this delightful dish
    1 banana
    Kiwi, mango, pineapple and berries
    3 small scoops frozen yogurt
    Top with Whip Cream
    1 cup *Canna* Nuts, chopped (Ch.8, pg.206-211)
Top with *Canna* whipped cream (Ch.10, pg. 283)

Nutty Avocado GF-Vegan

Dice	2 avocados
Drizzle with	1 tablespoon honey
Top with	¼ cup chopped *Canna* Nuts (Ch.8, pg.206-211)

Quinoa Blueberry Bar

Line a 9x13 inch baking pan with parchment paper and spray with cooking oil. Bake at 350°F for 5 minutes, cool and set aside
    1 cup rolled oats
    1 cup pecans, chopped
    ½ cup sesame seeds
Combine toasted oat mixture and toss with
    2 cups quinoa, puffed
    1 cup blueberries, dried
Bring to a boil, reduce heat and simmer for 5 minutes
    ½ cup honey
    ¼ cup molasses
    ¼ cup maple syrup
    ¼ cup stevia
    ¼ cup *Canna* Jelly Spice Butter (Ch.2, pg.30-31)
    1 *Canna Spicy Jelly Spice Blend*
    ½ cup butter
Remove from heat, add
    2 teaspoons vanilla extract
Pour honey mixture over quinoa and stir well. Press on to a parchment-lined baking sheet with a metal spatula, cover with another parchment and firmly press. Chill for 2 or more hours and place onto a work top and cut into long narrow bars. Refrigerate for 1 week or wrap tight and freeze. Bars are sticky unless chilled.

Kiwi Tart GF

Prepare 1 *Canna* Pie Crust (pg. 277-279), adding ½ cup crushed peanuts to the mix. Roll dough out and place in an ungreased tart or quiche pan, bake at 425°F for 15 minutes, cool.
Whisk until thickens
    1 cup sour cream
    1 vanilla pudding, instant sugar-free, small package
    1 cup *Canna* Milk (Ch.6, pg.138)
Remove cooled crust from pan and spread cream mixture into pie crust.
Arrange over cream
    3 cups kiwi, sliced
Heat over low until melted, cool
    ⅓ cup orange marmalade, sugar free
    2 tablespoons orange juice
Pour over kiwi and chill

Lemon Honey Sauce & Mangos GF-Vegan

Wisk together and heat for 15 minutes
    2 tablespoons coconut oil
    1 *Canna Lemon Pepper Spice Blend*
    2 tablespoons honey
    1 tablespoon lemon juice
Serve over sliced mangos

Rum Raisin Nut Sauce GF Vegan

Pour over bananas, pineapple, yogurt, sweet potatoes or lamb
Sauté for 15 minutes
    4 tablespoons coconut oil
    1 *Canna Spicy Jelly Spice Blend*
Add and continue to reduce, 5-10 minutes
    1 cup apple juice
    2 tablespoons xanthan gum
Toss in   ¼ cup *Canna* Rum (Ch.6, pg.142)
    ¾ cup raisins
    1 cup pecans, chopped

Ginger Bread Cookies

Combine 2¼ cups flour, whole wheat
 1 cup bran, toasted
 ⅓ cup stevia
 2 teaspoons baking soda
 2 teaspoons ginger, ground
 1 teaspoon salt

Mix in separate bowl
 1¾ cups butter
 1 *Canna Spicy Jelly Spice Blend*

Beat with mixer, then add all ingredients together
 2 eggs
 ½ cup molasses
 ½ cup stevia

Roll out between lightly floured parchments papers then refrigerate 5-10 minutes. Cut cookies and place on ungreased cookie sheet; top with pieces of chopped candied ginger. Bake at 325°F for 10-12 minutes. Make cookie dough ahead and store in refrigerator for up to 1 week.

Graham Nut Desert Topping Vegan

Combine and whisk over low heat
- 3 tablespoons butter, unsalted or coconut oil
- 1 *Canna Spicy Jelly Spice Blend*
- 2 tablespoons honey or stevia
- ½ teaspoon vanilla
- 1 tablespoon molasses

Combine in a separate bowl
- 2 tablespoons stevia
- ¼ cup graham flour
- 1 tablespoon flour, whole wheat
- 1 tablespoon bran
- ¾ teaspoon salt
- ½ cup *Canna* Nuts, chopped (Ch.8, pg.206-211)

Combine wet and dry mixtures, blending well. Spread onto a lined baking sheet. Bake at 325°F for 25 minutes until crispy golden brown, but not too dark. Cool.

Use as a topping for yogurt, ice cream and oatmeal

Zucchini-Walnut Loaf

Combine
- 1½ cups whole wheat flour
- 1 *Canna Spicy Jelly Spice Blend*
- 1 teaspoon baking powder
- ¼ teaspoon baking soda
- ¼ teaspoon salt

Whisk
- 2 large eggs, room temperature

Add and mix well
- 1 cup stevia
- ½ cup apple sauce, unsweetened
- 2 tablespoons coconut oil, softened
- 1 tablespoon lemon zest
- 1 cup zucchini, grated

Combine flour and egg mixture

Fold in   ½ cup *Canna* Walnuts, chopped (Ch.8, pg.206-211)

Bake in greased and floured loaf pan at 350°F for 1 hour or until knife comes out clean.

Chocolate & Cherries

Frozen Dark Cherries GF

Serve cherries over nonfat yogurt
Top with shaved dark chocolate and Whipped Cream

Chocolate Fondue GF

Heat over medium
- 2 cups heavy cream
- 1 *Canna Spicy Jelly Spice Blend*
- 3 tablespoons stevia

Pour over
- 16 ounces dark chocolate, broken in small pieces
- ⅓ cup *Canna* Spiced Rum

Stir slow, scraping sides and bottom until fully melted and combined.
Serve with colorful fruit

Chocolate Nut Bar Vegan

Melt over a double boiler
- 20 ounces dark baking chocolate
- 1 *Canna Spicy Jelly Spice Blend*
- ¼ cup coconut oil
- ¼ cup stevia
- 4 tablespoons vanilla

Pour onto rimmed lined cookie sheet
Top with   2 cups *Canna* Nuts, rough-chopped (Ch.8, pg.206-211)
Score into 2 inch squares and cool

Chocolate Peanut Drops Vegan

Microwave uncovered for 30 seconds
    2 cups dark chocolate chips
    ¼ cup stevia
Stir in and microwave for 30 seconds. Stir, microwave another 30 seconds
    ½ cup peanut butter
    1 *Canna Spicy Jelly Spice Blend*
Bake the chocolate and peanut butter on a cookie sheet at 350°F for 15 minutes before adding:
Add and stir   3½ cups sugar free fiber cereal, stir to coat
    1 cup peanuts
Drop by tablespoon onto wax paper and refrigerate until firm.

Chocolate Sauce GF

Place broken pieces in a warm pan on low until fully melted
    8 ounces unsweetened baking cocoa 65%
    1 *Canna Spicy Jelly Spice Blend*
Add and cook until bubbles begin
    1½ cups heavy cream
    3 tablespoons stevia
Remove from heat. Keep stirring until chocolate is smooth
Add   3 tablespoons butter, unsalted, softened
Add & stir   1 teaspoon vanilla extract
    ½ cup sour cream
    ¼ cup yogurt
    ¼ teaspoon baking soda

Serve warm or cool; seal and refrigerate.
Microwave for 30 seconds to soften. Do not overheat

Coconut Almond Bars GF-Vegan

Heat on low and Stir for 15 minutes
        3 tablespoons coconut oil
        1 *Canna Spicy Jelly Spice Blend*
Add   2 tablespoons xanthan gum
        2 cups coconut, shredded
        2 tablespoons stevia
Press onto a 9 inch parchment lined pan
Layer   1 cup almonds, chopped
Top with   1 cup dark chocolate pieces
Chill for 1 hour or more.
Cut into bars, wrap separately

Stuffed Sweet Dates GF

Heat 15 minutes, remove and cool
        2 tablespoons coconut oil
        1 *Canna Spicy Jelly Spice Blend*
        1 tablespoon stevia
Blend in   1 cup mascarpone cheese

Heat 5 minutes, cool for 15 minutes
Split and fill   12 dates

Frostings and Fillings

Bitter Sweet Cream filling GF

Heat for 10 minutes, blend, cool
    ¼ cup heavy cream
    1 *Canna Fruit Pie Spice Blend*
Beat until firm peaks form
    1 cup heavy cream
Add and beat Cooled Fruit Pie Cream
    1 teaspoon almond extract
    3 tablespoons stevia
Fold in   ½ cup Greek yogurt

Buttercream Frosting GF

In a saucepan over medium, whisk constantly until thickened.
    ½ cup water
    2 tablespoons powdered milk, nonfat
    3 tablespoons xanthan gum
Remove from heat and cool for 2 minutes
In a separate bowl, combine and whisk
    ⅓ cup *Canna* Butter (Ch.2, pg.31)
    2 tablespoons sour cream, fat free
    ¼ cup stevia
Stir in cooled milk
Add   2 teaspoons vanilla, whisk until light and fluffy.

Sweet Cream Cheese Filling GF

Heat on low for 15 minutes, cool,
    2 tablespoons butter, unsalted
    1 *Canna Fruit Pie Spice Blend*

Add and beat 4 ounces cream cheese, softened
    3 tablespoons stevia
    1 egg yolk
    1½ teaspoons vanilla
Place in a prepared pie crust and bake at 350°F for 25 minutes.

Quick Lemon Cream Filling GF

Heat for 10 minutes, cool
    ¼ cup heavy cream
    1 *Canna Fruit Pie Spice Blend*
    1 tablespoon stevia
Add and beat with an electric mixer
    11 ounces lemon curd, jar
    4 ounces cream cheese, softened
Serve as a side, topping or in a pre-baked pie shell.

Fruit and Canna Whipped Cream Dips GF
Sweet and simple, no fuss desert

Frozen red grapes, cantaloupe, guava and gogi berries
Top with *Canna* Whip Cream (Ch.10, pg. 283)

Maple Mascarpone GF

While whisking, simmer on low for 15 minutes. Cool
    ¼ cup heavy cream
    1 *Canna Fruit Pie Spice Blend*
Add in   ½ cup mascarpone cheese
    4 tablespoons maple syrup
    Spiced cream from above
    1 teaspoon lemon juice
Mix well and chill 1 hour
Serve as a sweet dip, topping or in a pre-baked pie shell.

Spicy Cream Whipped Frosting GF

Simmer on low for 15 minutes, cool.
    ½ cup heavy cream
    1 *Canna Fruit Pie Spice Blend*
Mix and microwave for 15 seconds to dissolve, cool
    1 packet gelatin, unflavored
    2 tablespoons water
Sprinkle over cooled cream and let stand 2 minutes
Whip in a separate, chilled bowl until peaks form
    1½ cups heavy cream
Add *Canna* Cream and continue whipping
Add   1 teaspoon vanilla
    3 tablespoons stevia

Quick Vanilla Cream Filling GF

Whisk together
    1 vanilla pudding pack, instant, sugar free
    2 tablespoons stevia
    1 cup sour cream
    1 cup *Canna* Milk (Ch.6, pg.138)
    1½ teaspoons vanilla
Serve alone, with fruit or in a baked pie crust

Jams

We break all of our rules when it comes to making jam. For all of the experimenting with jams and sugar substitutes I am never completely happy with the results. However, when I simply replace ½ of the sugar with stevia, the results are great!

This collection of *Canna* Jam recipes is for those who need to have *Canna* in all their food. The flavors of the cannabis and the concealing spices tend to overpower the soft flavors of the fruit, and therefore the results do not suit my taste.

Canna foodies really appreciate the alternative recipes, so here's to you!

Cherry Cranberry Chutney GF-Vegan

Bring to a boil, cover, reduce heat and simmer for 10 minutes
- 1 cup cranberries, dried
- 3 cups cherries, halved
- ¾ cup sweet cherry juice
- ½ cup stevia
- 1 *Canna Spicy Jelly Spice Blend*

Mash fruit, add
- ¼ cup lemon juice
- 4 teaspoons calcium water

In a separate bowl, combine
- ⅓ cup sugar
- 1 box pectin, low sugar

Bring fruit to a full boil, add slowly while stirring
- Sugar pectin mixture

Remove from the heat as soon as it comes to a full boil.
Using a canning funnel, pour into jars to ½ inch from the top. Clean rim and seal. Refrigerate for 24 hours. Freeze for up to 6 months.

Oregon Strawberry Jam GF-Vegan

Bring to boil and stir constantly for 1 minute
- 1 tablespoon butter or coconut oil
- 1 *Canna Spicy Jelly Spice Blend*
- ½ cup stevia
- ¼ cup sugar
- 1 box fruit pectin, no or low sugar
- ½ cup water

Remove from heat
Add and stir for 1 minute
- 4 cups strawberries, crushed

Using a canning funnel, pour into jars to ½ inch from the top. Clean rim and seal. Refrigerate for 24 hours. Freeze for up to 6 months.

Raspberry Mint Jam GF Vegan

Bring to a boil, lower the heat to medium-low for 20 minutes, cool
    1 tablespoon butter or coconut oil
    1 *Canna Spicy Jelly Spice Blend*
    1 cup mint, smashed
    1 cup grape juice, unsweetened
Mash and set aside
    3 cups raspberries
    1 tablespoon lemon juice
Boil for 1 minute
    ¾ cup grape juice, unsweetened
    1 package fruit pectin, low or sugar-free
Add, stirring constantly until fully dissolved
    ½ cup stevia
    ¼ cup sugar
    Mint sauce from above
Mix in berries; adjust sweetness for desired taste.

Using a canning funnel, pour into jars to ½ inch from the top. Clean rim and seal. Refrigerate for 24 hours. Freeze for up to 6 months.

Oregon Strawberry Topping -GF

Combine   1 teaspoon butter
    1 *Canna Spicy Jelly Spice Blend*
    ¼ cup stevia
    ¼ cup sugar
Add, bring to boil, stirring constantly for 1 minute; remove from heat.
Add   1 pectin box, low or sugar-free
    ½ cup water
Add and stir 1 minute
    6 cups strawberries, crushed

Using a canning funnel, pour into jars to ½ inch from the top. Clean rim and seal. Refrigerate 24 hours. Freeze for up to 6 months.

Blueberry Jam GF-Vegan

Mash
        3 cups blueberries
        1 tablespoon lemon juice

Boil for 1 minute
        1¾ cups grape juice, unsweetened
        1 teaspoon butter or coconut oil
        1 package fruit pectin, sugar-free

Add and stir constantly until fully dissolved
        1 *Canna Spicy Jelly Spice Blend*
        ½ cup stevia
        ¼ cup sugar

Mix in berries, adjusting the sweetness as needed

Using a canning funnel, pour into jars to ½ inch from the top. Clean rim and seal. Refrigerate 24 hours. Freeze for up to 6 months.

NOTES

Pie Crusts

Almond Crust GF-Vegan

Mix   1½ cup almond meal
               3 teaspoons *Canna* Fruit Pie Spice Butter or coconut oil (Ch.2, pg.31-32)
               2 teaspoons stevia

Press into pie or tart pan. For a fully pre baked shell, bake for 15 minutes at 350°F, add filling. For a crust that will require baking after the filling is added, bake for 10 minutes, fill and continue baking following the filling directions.

Quick Bran Pie Crust Vegan

Mix in pie pan
               ¾ cup flour, whole wheat
               ¼ cup wheat bran
               2 teaspoons stevia
               ¼ teaspoon salt
Combine   ⅓ cup *Canna* Italian Olive Oil (Ch.2, pg.32)
               3 tablespoons ice water

While mixing the flour, slowly add oil mixture; blend well with a fork then press into pan.
For a fully pre baked shell, bake for 15 minutes at 350°F, add filling. For a crust that will require baking after the filling is added, bake for 10 minutes, fill and continue baking following the filling directions.

Quick Pie Crust Vegan

Mix in pie pan 1 cup flour, whole wheat
               ¼ teaspoon salt
Mix well with a fork in a separate bowl
               ⅓ cup *Canna* Spicy Jelly Oil or butter (Ch.2, pg.32)
               3 tablespoons ice water

While mixing the flour slowly in the pie pan, add the oil mixture; blend well then press into pie pan.
For a fully pre baked shell, bake for 15 minutes at 350°F, add filling. For a crust that will require baking after the filling is added, bake for 10 minutes, fill and continue baking following the filling directions.

Fiber Pie Crust Vegan

Mix   2 cups fiber cereal, fiber or buds (not flakes)
⅓ cup *Canna* Fruit Pie Coconut Oil, softened (Ch.2, pg.32)
1 tablespoon stevia
1 teaspoon vanilla

Blend all ingredients before pressing into pie pan.
For a fully pre-baked shell, bake for 15 minutes at 350°F, add filling. For a crust that will require baking after the filling is added, bake for 10 minutes. Fill and continue baking following the filling directions.

Quick Graham-Bran Pie Crust Vegan

Mix   ¾ cup graham cracker crumbs
¼ cup wheat bran

Melt until dissolved, set aside
5 tablespoons *Canna* Spicy Jelly Butter or coconut oil (Ch.2, pg.31-32)
1 tablespoons stevia

Add all together and mix well with a fork, press into pan and prick.
For a fully pre baked shell, bake for 15 minutes at 350°F, add filling. For a crust that will require baking after the filling is added, bake for 10 minutes, fill and continue baking following the filling directions.

Pumpkin Pie No Crust GF

Combine   15 ounce pumpkin, canned
⅓ cup stevia
2 tablespoons honey
1 *Canna Spicy Jelly Spice Blend*

Add   2 eggs, lightly beaten
1 teaspoon vanilla

Gradually add ¾ cup evaporated milk
Pour into a lightly greased 8-inch spring form pan, on a foil lined tray.
Bake at 325°F 45-50 minutes until sets. Cool 1 hour and cover another 2 hours or more. Serve with whipped cream.

Finish with   1½ cups *Canna* Honey Pecans, chopped (Ch.8, pg.211)

Canna Popsicles

Mix, blend and pour into molds. Freeze for 8 hours

Banana Pops GF

½ cup *Canna* Milk, fat free (Ch.6, pg.138)
4 smashed bananas
¼ cup stevia
½ cup *Canna* Peanut butter, smooth (Ch.2, pg.31-32)
Pinch of salt
¼ cup honey

Coconut Pops GF

1 14 ounce coconut milk, canned
1 cup *Canna* Cream (Ch.6, pg.139)
¼ cup stevia
2 tablespoons limeade concentrate
1 tablespoon lime zest
2 tablespoons lemon juice
Pinch of salt

Pineapple Pops GF-Vegan

Mix and marinate for 24 hours
    1 cup pineapple juice
    1 cup crushed pineapple
    1 *Canna Spicy Jelly Spice Blend*

Add & mix
    1 mango, diced small
    ½ cup honey
    2 tablespoons lemon juice

Pinch of salt

Yogurt Parfaits

Flavored Yogurt Parfait GF

Whisk well to dissolve
    1 cup yogurt, plain
    ¼ teaspoon almond, orange or vanilla extract
    1 teaspoon stevia

Lemon Fruit Pie Parfait GF 4 servings

Heat on low for 10 minutes, set aside to cool
    3 tablespoons coconut oil
    1 *Canna Fruit Pie Spice Blend*
    2 teaspoons stevia
Whisk into cooled oil
    4 cups yogurt
    1 tablespoon lemon juice
Alternate with spiced yogurt
    1 cup colorful fruits
Top with   Whipped Cream (Pg.283)

Parfait Toppings GF-Vegan

    2 tablespoons dark chocolate, shaved
    1 tablespoon *Canna* Honey Nuts (Ch.8, pg.206-211)
    Sprinkle of stevia

    1 teaspoon honey
    1¾ cup blueberries
    Top with *Canna* Honey Almonds

    ¾ cup strawberries, sliced,
    2 tablespoons dark chocolate, shaved
    Sprinkle of stevia
    1 tablespoon *Canna* Nuts

Strawberries & Cream

Whisk and bring to a soft boil for 5-10 minutes
    2 cups heavy cream
    1 *Canna Fruit Pie Spice Blend*
    2 tablespoons stevia
Place in a cocktail glass and float in cream mixture
    4 cups strawberries
Top with shaved dark chocolate and Whipped Cream (Pg.283)

Watermelon Parfait

Cube watermelon into 1 inch pieces
Add 1 dollop of *Canna* Whip Cream Frosting to each serving (Pg.283)
Top with strawberries, blueberries and mint leaves

Whipped Creams

Whipped Cream GF

Beat until peaks form
        2 cups heavy cream
Add   ¼ cup stevia
        1 teaspoon vanilla

Spiced Cream Frosting GF

Simmer on low for 15 minutes, set aside
        ½ cup heavy cream
        1 *Canna Fruit Pie Spice Blend*
        ¼ cup stevia
Combine and microwave for 15 seconds, stir until dissolved
        1 gelatin pack, unflavored
        2 tablespoons water
Let stand 2 minutes until cool to the touch
Whip in chilled bowl until peaks form
        1½ cups heavy cream
Slowly add and whip together
        1 teaspoon vanilla
        Cooled gelatin
Fold in *Canna* Cream and continue to whip for 10 seconds

Spiced Cranberry Cream GF

Heat for 10 minutes on low, chill
        1 *Canna Fruit Pie Spice Blend*
        ½ cup cranberries, dried and chopped
        ½ cup heavy cream
        ¼ cup stevia
Beat until peaks form
        2 cups heavy cream
Add   ¼ cup stevia
        1 teaspoon vanilla
Fold cranberry cream into whipped cream

NOTES

REFERENCES

The following sites are among the many
we've used in our research.

- activehealth.ie
- articles.mercola.com
- bulletproofexec.com
- caloriecount.com
- calorieking.com
- care2.com
- chicagotribune.com
- dogsnaturallymagazine.com
- draxe.com
- drweil.com
- examiner.com
- foodsafetynews.com
- foodservicewarehouse.com
- globalhealingcenter.com
- gracelinks.org
- health.com
- huffingtonpost.com
- insightsinipf.com
- mensfitness.com
- naturalhomeremedies.com
- newsmedical.net
- nourishingplot.com
- nutritiondata.self.com
- parkinsons.about.com
- petmd.com
- rheumatoidarthritis.net
- sparkpeople.com
- starwestbotanicals.com
- teatoxify.com
- themacateam.com
- truenutrition.com
- uchospitals.edu
- vega-licious.com
- vegkitchen.com
- webmd.com
- webmed.com
- whfoods.com
- wholehealthchicago.com

www.ingramcontent.com/pod-product-compliance
Lightning Source LLC
Chambersburg PA
CBHW042129010526
44111CB00031B/32